Facilitating Workshops

Palgrave Teaching and Learning

Series Editor: **Sally Brown**

Facilitating Workshops
For the Love of Learning
Leading Dynamic Seminars
Live Online Learning

Further titles are in preparation

Universities into the 21st Century

Series Editors: **Noel Entwistle and Roger King**

Becoming an Academic
Cultures and Change in Higher Education
Global Inequalities in Higher Education
Learning Development in Higher Education
Managing Your Academic Career
Managing Your Career in Higher Education Administration
Research and Teaching
Teaching Academic Writing in UK Higher Education
Teaching for Understanding at University
Understanding the International Student Experience
The University in the Global Age
Writing in the Disciplines

Palgrave Research Skills

Authoring a PhD
The Foundations of Research (2nd edn)
Getting to Grips with Doctoral Research
The Good Supervisor (2nd edn)
Maximizing the Impacts of University Research
The Postgraduate Research Handbook (2nd edn)
The Professional Doctorate
Structuring Your Research Thesis

You may also be interested in:

Teaching Study Skills and Supporting Learning

For a complete listing of all our titles in this area please visit
www.palgrave.com/studyskills

Facilitating Workshops

A Resource Book for Lecturers and Trainers

Hayo Reinders
Marilyn Lewis

palgrave
macmillan

First published 2014 by
PALGRAVE MACMILLAN

Palgrave Macmillan in the UK is an imprint of Macmillan Publishers Limited, registered in England, company number 785998, of Houndmills, Basingstoke, Hampshire RG21 6XS.

Palgrave Macmillan in the US is a division of St Martin's Press LLC, 175 Fifth Avenue, New York, NY 10010.

Palgrave Macmillan is the global academic imprint of the above companies and has companies and representatives throughout the world.

Palgrave® and Macmillan® are registered trademarks in the United States, the United Kingdom, Europe and other countries

ISBN: 978–1–137–30420–9 paperback

This book is printed on paper suitable for recycling and made from fully managed and sustained forest sources. Logging, pulping and manufacturing processes are expected to conform to the environmental regulations of the country of origin.

A catalogue record for this book is available from the British Library.

A catalog record for this book is available from the Library of Congress.

Typeset by Cambrian Typesetters, Camberley, Surrey

Printed in China

From Marilyn

To the next generation of child writers with the name Lewis.

From Hayo

*To Sang-Yeong and Ul-Soon Kim,
the best in-laws in the world.*

Contents

Notes on the authors

Dr Hayo Reinders (www.innovationinteaching.org) is Head of Education at Unitec in New Zealand and TESOL Professor and Director of the doctoral program at Anaheim University in the United States. He is also Editor-in-Chief of Innovation in Language Learning and Teaching. Hayo's interests are in technology in education, learner autonomy, and out-of-class learning and he is a speaker on these subjects for the Royal Society of New Zealand. His most recent books are on teacher autonomy, teaching methodologies, and second language acquisition and he edits a book series on 'New Language Learning and Teaching Environments' for Palgrave Macmillan.

Marilyn Lewis is an honorary research fellow at the University of Auckland with special interests in language teaching and teacher education. She enjoys writing books and articles and conducting workshops in New Zealand and Asia.

List of figures and tables

Acknowledgements

Our vignettes were supplied by many people. Some wanted to remain anonymous, others wanted us to edit and modify what they wrote and still others modestly told us to omit them if they were no good. Thanks to all of you.

Thanks to Perceptia Press (www.perceptiapress.com) for giving permission to use the figure on page 18.

Thanks to Charles C. Thomas, Publisher Ltd, for giving permission to use the material on pages 43–7.

Series editor's preface

This new series of books with Palgrave, for all who care about teaching and learning in higher education, is launched with the express aim of providing useful, relevant, current and helpful guidance on key issues in learning and teaching in the tertiary/post-compulsory education sector. This is an area of current very rapid and unpredictable change, with universities and colleges reviewing and often implementing radical alterations in the ways they design, deliver and assess the curriculum, taking into account not just innovations in how content is being delivered and supported, particularly through technological means, but also the changing relationships between academics and their students. The role of the teacher in higher education needs to be reconsidered when students can freely access content worldwide and seek accreditation and recognition of learning by local, national or international providers (and may indeed prefer to do so). Students internationally are becoming progressively more liable for the payment of fees, as higher education comes to be seen less as a public good and more as a private one, and this too changes the nature of the transaction.

Texts in this series will address these and other emergent imperatives. Among topics covered, volumes will explore student-centred approaches at undergraduate and post-graduate levels including doctoral work, the necessity to work in an internationalised and transnational, tertiary education context, the challenges of staff–student interactions where engagements are as likely to be through new technologies as face-to-face in the classroom, and issues about the levels of student engagement, especially where study is in competition with other demands on their time including employment and caring responsibilities. This text on *Facilitating Workshops* provides a welcome contribution to the series.

Sally Brown
October 2013

Introduction to the book

When the idea for this book first emerged during one of our official meetings (read: coffee breaks), we thought it would be, if not easy to write, then certainly straightforward. Surely with our combined experience working and teaching in different countries we knew what there was to say about facilitating workshops? Of course, as so often happens, the more we thought and wrote about the topic, the more we realised we had much to learn ourselves. Especially once we started probing our colleagues, participants and random members of the public for their experiences, we humbly revised our original expectation. The range of learning and teaching contexts, materials, customs and activities used in different countries and industries is very broad indeed.

We have done our best to take this wide range of ideas, knowledge and experiences and integrate it into this book. We have done this by including on the one hand as many different situations and examples as possible, and on the other the voices of those who have so kindly offered to share their words of wisdom. You will find a range of quotes, anecdotes and questions scattered throughout the book, and indeed we suggest that for some readers these will be the most useful way to find those sections that are most relevant to them. For this reason, in addition to a regular table of contents and an index, we have included a 'map' of common questions and workshop concerns at the start of the book. Simply find those you identify with most and go to those sections of the book where the issue is dealt with.

This is a book by practitioners for practitioners. We have strived to make the text approachable and the examples relevant to real-life situations. It is our belief that an understanding of the theory underlying good practice (and the impact of good practice on theory-building) is essential, if not for preparing tomorrow's workshop, then certainly for one's own personal and professional development in the long term. For this reason, we make frequent references to learning and teaching theories, and the first part of the book deals with the background to successful workshops in general.

You may notice a change in tone between Parts 1, 2 and 3. Whereas Part 1 is predominantly theoretical and based on other people's ideas, research and theories, Part 2 and, to an even greater extent, Part 3 are based on our own and other facilitators' experiences, concerns and questions. As a result you may find the language in Part 1 more formal and technical, compared with the more personal style in Part 3 in particular.

It is our sincere hope that you will find this book inspiring, that you will find comfort in the knowledge that others have struggled with the same questions as you face, and that through our and others' experiences and ideas you will feel confident and motivated to explore the fascinating and unique environment offered in workshops.

Hayo Reinders and Marilyn Lewis
Bangkok and Auckland, 2013

Common questions and workshop concerns

In this first section we list a number of complaints we have heard about workshops. Following each complaint we indicate the section of the book where this concern is addressed. You can use this list as an alternative to the index or table of contents.

▶ Part 1 Learning in workshops

At the conference, I deliberately chose a mixture of talks and workshops. To my disappointment many of the so-called 'workshops' turned out actually to be talks. Don't presenters get sent a list of guidelines on how to run workshops?

See: Why workshops? Or: Defining a workshop

As a matter of interest, who first thought up the name 'workshop'? Does it have a definition? I've been to all sorts of these events labelled 'workshops' in the course of my professional life and it's hard to see that some of them have anything in common.

See: A brief history of workshops

I've noticed that workshop presenters often act as if there's just one kind of learner. One presenter might have all the activities going, from a theoretical point to an example, while another does the opposite. There might be differences from one workshop to the next but not within one workshop. Surely it's possible to give some choice when it comes to activities?

See: Principles of adult learning

Workshop presenters should look round the room during activity time and count the number of glazed over eyes. That would tell them more about the engagement of participants than reading the evaluation sheets later.

See: Motivation

3

Some of the best workshops I've been to were the ones where the presenter made a deliberate effort to make everyone feel at ease. But too often, workshop facilitators seem to have no regard for people's feelings. They could improve things, for example, by realising that not everyone feels comfortable talking in front of others from the first minute.

See: Affect

Although I respect most presenters' vast knowledge and experience, some don't seem to think participants have any experience of their own or can think for themselves. Let's face it, most of the learning will have to happen after the workshop, so it would be good if presenters could focus more on the collective knowledge and experience of the group.

See: Learner autonomy

One thing that really annoys me after the suggestion to 'Get into groups and discuss …' is the instruction, 'Remember to move around the room and not just talk to the person beside you.' Why not? We are usually sitting with people whose company we enjoy. What's wrong with that? We are not children to be told who to talk to.

See: Adults as social learners

It's all very well being shown how to do something and told why the demonstrator is doing such and such, but what's wrong with letting us try things out for ourselves? It's tiresome to hear the person say, 'If we had more time/equipment space we could try this out, but as it is …' We paid to go to this workshop. They should have hired a place with enough equipment for us to have a go.

See: Adults as experiential learners

▶ Part 2 Teaching in workshops

What really trips me up is how to organise the content and the activities in such a way that it all comes together in the end, especially because you do want to leave some room for flexibility as well.

See: Planning and organising workshops

I'm speaking here as an organiser. We were told that we'd have to get to a certain venue for the workshop, which I took to mean that the facilities there were better than ours or perhaps that people were coming from other workplaces. No such thing. We were the only people there and the facilities were inferior to what we could offer. What's more, we had to hire a bus, not to mention the cost of the travelling time.

See: Workshop contexts

I once made the mistake of overconfidently offering to deliver a workshop online when I was not able to travel. Everything went wrong, from poor sound, to a lost internet connection, to a chaotic tangle of messages from participants that I didn't know how to handle. Clearly, I'd need to prepare much better next time.

See: Delivering workshops online

I've noticed that some presenters announce grandiose goals for a workshop which are quite unrealistic given the time available. Maybe there should be two sorts of goals: short-term and long-term.

See: Setting goals

One of my gripes is that so many workshop activities are childish. I don't necessarily mean the content, but the process certainly is.

See: Stages of learning

One of the hardest things for me about organising good workshops is knowing what activities to select and how to sequence them in such a way that there is a meaningful progression.

See: Categorising and selecting activities

I've always disliked role-plays but see that some presenters are using them successfully in their workshops. I think I was sometimes put off by language like 'Let's pretend'. Role-plays are much more than pretending.

See: Role-play

There is so much talk these days of how popular games are, and some are starting to use them in their workshops. I wonder how they do this so that it's not just entertainment, but actual education.

See: Demonstrations, performances and games

Do I start with an easy task so that I can slowly progress to more difficult ones, or do I start with a harder task to motivate the participants to want to learn more?

See: Sequencing content and activities

Everything I learned about giving workshops I learned by observing others and making lots of mistakes. There must be a more efficient way.

See: Professional development for facilitators

▶ **Part 3 The practice of facilitating workshops**

The last time I offered a workshop it was on a Friday afternoon. The feedback from the participants was that they were too tired and would have preferred it on another day. This time I gave the workshop on a Monday but now participants said they were too worried about all the week's tasks ahead. Is there a right time for workshops?

See: The 'when' of workshops

The other day I was asked to do an introductory workshop for our human resources team on dealing with complaints. It is a very difficult topic and I normally spend at least a full day on it. The organisers, however, were adamant that the workshop should last two hours maximum. I really struggled to make it a meaningful experience for the participants.

See: Timing issues

I'd be interested to hear what other people do when they've been told to prepare for a workshop of 20 people but, when the time comes, there are twice that number clamouring at the door. Whose responsibility is it to turn people away?

See: How many participants is right?

Sometimes I see people yawning, or even falling asleep. It always really unsettles me. I immediately think I must be a terrible presenter. Do others feel like this too?

See: Handling signs of boredom

The range of people I've seen in workshops is staggering. How do presenters deal with such diversity?

See: Different types of participants

My problem is timing the breaks during the workshops. Sometimes the coordinator tells me ahead of time that we must have breaks at such and such a time because that's when the catering staff prepare food and drinks. When the time comes, at that very moment we could be in the middle of an activity.

See: Handling breaks

I'm never quite sure what to do at the end of the workshop to end it in the 'right' way. The ending sometimes seems slightly awkward.

See: Closing

Do I need to use the latest software to give a good workshop? Sometimes I wonder if I am just being lazy not to keep up with all the latest technologies. How do I know what is worthwhile using in class?

See: Technical issues

I have noticed as a participant that I learn much better in some environments than others. How do I create a space that is most conducive to learning?

See: What is the optimal environment for a workshop?

The other day I arrived in this horrible little room, with fixed desks in rows. I was glad to get out after the three-hour workshop. I think the participants were, too. What else could I have done but make the best of it?

See: Inadequate seating

Although so much information is available online, I actually find it surprisingly hard to find specific materials that are suitable for particular groups. How do others find good resources?

See: Content issues

We had a mixture of presenters at our workshop and it was quite clear who was accustomed to this kind of event and who was new to it. Is it fair to a new presenter to be matched with someone so much better or is that seen as a kind of training process?

See: First time facilitating

Has anyone else come across this one? I took the workshop handout back to my workplace to show it round. Someone said, 'That's not hers. It comes from ...' and she went and found the book it had been taken from.

See: Copyright and privacy issues

My nightmare scenario came true the other day; I had spent ages preparing a workshop for a group of nurses who, I was told, needed to learn how to 'handle difficult conversations with patients'. It turned out that a few weeks earlier a nurse had been badly attacked by an angry patient and they were expecting to be taught how to defend themselves. I made the most of it, but it was not my finest hour. How could I have avoided this?

See: Mismatch between participants' levels, goals and actual needs

Workshops take participants' time and money. It's not enough for them to go away thinking it's been fun and a chance to meet interesting people. I want them to have something more than that to get their teeth into and to report back to others.

See: Too much or too little content

The topic I've been asked to address is really not my strength. I don't want to seem difficult but I would rather cover a different topic. How can I suggest this?

See: Negotiating content

I've had both situations where the hosts wanted me to offer a workshop that was far too short for the subject, and cases where the opposite was true. How can I handle situations like this?

See: Negotiating the length of the workshop

I am a teacher, not a business person. I really have no idea how much to ask for. What is reasonable?

See: Negotiating remuneration

I used to be so delighted to be invited that I'd say yes every time. I've learned the hard way that it doesn't do your professional image any good to try and make your topic fit some unsuitable demands.

See: Declining invitations

I have been considering running my own workshops as I usually end up doing all the work anyway. What should I think about?

See: Organising your own workshops

It would be good if organisers didn't have a 'one size fits all' advertisement for their workshops. I don't know how many times my staff come back and say, 'You told us they'd ... and they didn't.' I'd like to say it's dishonest, but more likely it's just careless.

See: Promoting workshops

At almost every workshop I have attended or organised there is the obligatory 'feedback form'. I have never quite understood the point of this. Where do the results go, and what is done with them?

See: Evaluating workshops

I recently went on a two-week course on financial reporting. When I came back, my supervisor asked me to give a workshop to the rest of the accounting department. I feel very awkward. These are the people I work with every day and now suddenly I have to teach them. What will they think of me?

See: Giving workshops to colleagues

PART 1
Learning in workshops

Why workshops?

A number of reasons have been put forward for choosing a workshop over a lecture or a series of readings as a form of professional development. The case for using workshops as a way of giving new knowledge skills and attitudes has been summarised by Richards and Farrell (2005) in relation to one group of professionals: language teachers. Since most of the points they make can apply to workshops in general, we now use their points as headings.

Input from experts

People organising workshops often look beyond their own workplace for presenters who are seen as experts. By 'expert' they may mean someone who is well known in the field or who has developed some fresh ideas. Certainly if someone's name is well known to potential workshop attenders, then this can be a drawcard. But what do people understand by the word 'expert'?

According to the *Cambridge Advanced Learner's Dictionary*, an expert is 'a person with a high level of knowledge or skill'. As if to counter the thought that this must equal advanced qualifications, they give the following example. '*My mother is an expert at dressmaking* = she does it very well'. People may be drawn to a workshop because of a big name, but unless the person turns out to be someone who can 'do' the thing well, attenders are likely to be unsatisfied.

Traditionally the input was brought physically by the expert to the workshop, but technology has now reached the point where, with careful planning, one or more people can appear on the screen at different times during the day, as we shall see in the section on 'Delivering workshops online' (p. 123). In this case, they may not actually organise the whole day, but they do give input which informs and inspires.

Practical applications

A second feature of workshops mentioned by Richards and Farrell is that they offer practical applications of theory. While the experts referred to above may bring knowledge to the workshop, unless participants take away ideas which are relevant to their daily work, the final evaluations may not be favourable. There are various ways of making sure that practical applications can happen.

The input sessions may be separated from the applications by moving participants from one space to another where some practical work can be done. This can apply to topics as diverse as computer systems and farm equipment. During these practical parts, there may be more than one person available to give participants individual feedback on their practice. For some topics, safety requirements mean that the practice cannot be in an actual workplace. Thus transport providers such as bus companies or airlines will often spend part of the workshop teaching drivers and pilots using simulators.

Another way of practising real-life applications is through role-plays, as we shall see in the section on 'Role-play' (p. 109).

Motivation

There are many reasons why workshops can be motivating, starting with the fact that they are a break from the daily routine. Even being selected to attend the workshop may be motivating, if it is presented as something offered to staff who are already successful. Motivation also comes from meeting attenders from other workplaces. Group activities, such as those suggested in the section on 'Motivation' (p. 24), provide the chance for exchanges that go beyond the social.

Trivial as it may sound, motivation also comes from such details as the ambience of the meeting place and the provision of refreshments during the breaks. The interactions during these breaks can be an important motivator, the break being a time to set up contacts which go beyond the workshop.

The topic of motivation is revisited in the section on 'Motivation' (p. 24).

Collegiality

As mentioned, relations with colleagues can be built up in a way that is impossible in the daily routine. There can be other unexpected bonuses too, as this first-hand account shows.

'Not everyone was pleased to notice that X was one of the people from our workplace chosen to attend a workshop in a distant location. They doubted that she would have much to contribute and she might not even be a good advertisement for our firm.

How wrong we were! In a different setting we saw this person in a fresh light. She had strengths that we had never noticed but which were spotted by the workshop facilitator. Our time away made a difference to workplace relationships when we all returned the following week.'

Innovations

It is common in a workplace for some people to embrace change while others resist it. When time is spent at a workshop answering objections and showing advantages, innovations can be seen in a different light. It may be unrealistic to imagine that everyone will go back convinced that the changes are a good thing, but there is more likelihood of greater understanding.

Short-term

Whereas some forms of professional development involve participants in taking lengthy time off for study, the advantage of workshops is that they are short. Ideally they cause little disruption at the workplace. This is an advantage financially as well as in other ways.

Flexibility

From the perspective of the presenter, workshops are flexible. Typically, presenters are asked to deal with topics on which they have run workshops before. However, this doesn't mean that the content or formats are identical. This is how one presenter puts it.

'Usually the invitation comes because people have heard about a previous workshop I have run somewhere else. However, I try not to have exactly the same input in each place, and certainly not the same flow to the time. Ideally they give me information beforehand about who is coming, so that I can tailor things to suit that group. If there are some surprises on arrival, at least I can play around with the order of the activities or the balance of time for input and application.'

Active learning

One further reason, not mentioned in the list from Richards and Farrell (2005) and perhaps the strongest for using the workshop format for introducing new ideas, is the belief that people learn better through active than through receptive learning. Yet even when lecturers or speakers believe this to be true, they do not always match their actions to their beliefs. This was shown in the results of one survey carried out by a tertiary teacher trainer. Some days before the lecturers were due to attend a workshop, she sent out a short questionnaire with three items. Here are the questions, with the teachers' responses:

1 *What percentage of class time do you spend lecturing?*
   ANSWER:
   Average: 70%
2 *Besides lectures, do you use any other methods to teach? If so, what methods do you use? Please list them below.*
   ANSWERS:
   Top three answers were: discussion (19 teachers), use of visual aids (11 teachers), case analysis (9 teachers). (I wouldn't call the second a method, but I'm not going to get into that at this point.)
       Most of the 24 methods they listed are methods that I would say get students involved in the process of learning. But of those methods, more than half were what I would call vague or non-specific ideas, such as participation, interaction, sharing, dialogue.
3 *On a scale of 1 to 10, with 1 being a lot less and 10 being much more, do you feel students learn less, just as much, or more, when you use other methods rather than a more traditional (lecture) approach?*
   ANSWER:
   Average ... 7 (so they believe students learn more from other methods).

The workshop presenter saw a gap between what teachers believe and what they do. They believe other methods, those that get students involved in the process of learning, to be more effective, but they still mostly lecture.

She wondered whether the gap between what they believe and what they do might exist because they don't know how to turn vague ideas into specific applications. Announcing these results at the start of her workshop would help attenders to see the point of the activities she planned to introduce.

To workshop or not to workshop

There are situations where workshops offer the ideal type of activity, and equally there are cases where a lecture or presentation may be more suited.

▶ Where time is very short. Workshops are more time-consuming than presentations, for the same amount of content.
▶ With large numbers. Although workshops with large audiences are possible (see 'Too many or too few participants', p. 148), this is not ideal.
▶ Where participants do not expect it. At an event for possible investors in a new venture, participants simply expecting to be given facts and projections will not be amused if asked to join in a workshop.

▶ Where the facilities do not allow it. Although in most cases a way can be found to work-around this, there are situations where cramped space, or a noisy environment (or one where neighbouring rooms would be disturbed by noise from the workshop), simply militate against using workshops.

▶ For diplomatic reasons. One of us sometimes teaches government officials, including both junior and very senior staff, and first meetings usually take place using a more formal format.

A brief history of workshops

► **Defining a workshop**

To most people, the word 'workshop' conjures up an image of a session where participants do as much work as the presenter. Interestingly enough, current definitions often focus more on the content and the purpose than on details of the process. For Richards and Farrell (2005: 23), 'A workshop is an intensive, short-term learning activity that is designed to provide an opportunity to acquire specific knowledge and skills.'

In the introduction to their edited collection aimed at teacher educators, Freeman and Cornwell (1993) describe the activities in their book as the opposite of 'the knowledge-transmission model of education' (p. xiii). Their contributors 'resist the assumption that people will learn to teach just by being told what to do or how to do it' (ibid.). Workshops are based on this same principle. The learning happens as attenders work to build up their own understanding of the topic being presented. An important element in this is interaction, as shown in the model in Figure 1.1, by Reinders, Lewis and Kirkness (2010: 37).

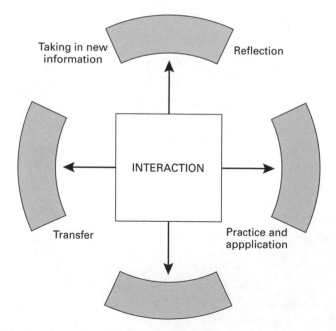

Figure 1.1 The place of interaction in workshops

Table 1.1 Skills and workshop activities

Skill	Workshop activity
Knowledge	Put an idea into your own words for others, e.g. design a poster with a slogan.
Comprehension	Explain a new idea as if to colleagues who haven't attended the workshop, e.g. a 3-minute presentation.
Application	Go from theory to practice, e.g. group brainstorm ways of applying a new idea to various workplaces.
Analysis	Compare and contrast, e.g. draw up a list of similarities and differences between the familiar and the new ideas.

Assuming, as the diagram does, that a workshop involves people in thinking or reflecting on the new ideas being presented to them, it is helpful to consider that different workshop activities involve varying levels of engagement and understanding on the part of the participants. Bloom's Taxonomy of learning activities was designed to answer the question: 'What does it mean exactly to have a full grasp of a new topic, and be able to use your learning successfully even in new situations?' (from Petty, 2004: 7). Based on Petty's summary, Table 1.1 lists some suggestions for workshop activities which move from the 'relatively undemanding ... [to the] more difficult ... and much more useful' (p. 8).

The workshop experience

Leaving aside for the moment the complaint sometimes voiced at a conference that a particular workshop session was no different from a lecture, we now consider the type of activity that can be offered to workshop attenders. One format is:

Observe > analyse > practise > apply

The observation phase may be a physical observation, such as a visit to a workplace to see workers in their own setting, or it may be a DVD with video recordings of relevant professional situations. In the latter case, the stages can be interwoven, as the presenter stops the recording from time to time while participants are guided to analyse what is happening. Of course, the observation need not be of the process. Workshop participants could be shown products. In the case of a business workplace, the product could be a business plan. Following a guided analysis of this plan, the presenter could lead participants towards designing a business plan of their own. A hypothetical plan based on a case study would allow practice, until finally the principles are applied to the actual workplace of the workshop participants.

Why attend a workshop?

Workshops can have a number of purposes or intended outcomes. One workshop could achieve several of these simultaneously.

1 Team building

Team building has been said to have various purposes, for example: 'to improve self-understanding, build trust and enhance interpersonal communication' (Portell, 2012). However, as Portell points out, cultural differences may mean that not all workshop activities translate easily from one country, or group of participants, to another. Her experience of conducting workshops in Mongolia makes her advice here particularly relevant.

2 Introducing staff to innovations

Another common reason for holding workshops is because something new is about to be introduced. The innovation may be something tangible such as a computer system or a new piece of equipment, but it could also be a new way of doing something, such as the procedures for conducting R&D.

3 Professional updating

This purpose is slightly different from the last, in that there may not be anything radically new to explain and learn. It may simply be that staff have become a little tired or careless or traditional, and need to be inspired with new ideas. This type of workshop can often include amongst its presenters someone from a related workplace, who shows participants what they are doing.

Principles of adult learning

Underpinning all the preparation that goes into workshops are general principles of learning. Because this book concerns working with adults, we do not include the general literature on learning that includes children's education. Instead we focus on the way adults learn and, flowing from that, the way people teach when their 'audience' is made up of adults. Of course, the word 'audience' is not well chosen when our topic is workshops. Even more than in regular classrooms, the emphasis when preparing workshops is to build on the way people learn. The 'teaching' is probably better referred to as 'facilitating learning'.

In this first part of the book, we deal with various aspects of adult learning, in particular the way they might be reflected in the preparation of workshops.

▶ Individual differences

The following true story relates to a computer workshop from the 1980s, when computers were starting to be provided for all members of the work force to use as an alternative to handing in pages of longhand to the secretary for typing. As encouragement to staff to use these new tools, they were given time off weekly for a training session in the computer suite (see the following vignette).

VIGNETTE

'There were three attenders at the workshop, all of whom could type. The facilitator, who was also their colleague, sat them down, each in front of one screen, and then started to deliver a mini-lecture on the history of computing. A few minutes later, perhaps sensing some boredom, he said he would start demonstrating.

"Everyone watch me. You'll notice that I ... ." He then gave a running commentary on what he was doing.

One of the participants quietly started to imitate him, using the computer in front of her. He quickly stopped her.

"Don't start yet. You might make a mistake and then you'd feel foolish." '

Underlying the facilitator's genuine concern for the wayward workshop attender was the thought that making mistakes is embarrassing. The participant, on the other hand, expected to make mistakes, planned to learn from them and would certainly not have beeen embarrassed by them. The presenter seemed not to like learning by trial and error himself, and had a strong sense of the importance of keeping up appearances.

What does this anecdote tell us? Whereas a fixed input, such as listening to a lecture, watching a DVD or reading an article, caters for just one way of learning, workshops are ideally suited to offering alternatives during the sessions instead of making everyone march to the same tune. However, some organisers still act as if everyone learned in the same way.

The different ways in which people learn have been described many times in relation to both children and adults. Nearly thirty years ago, Biggs and Telfer (1987: 409) quoted a late seventeenth-century source (John Locke, *Some Thoughts Concerning Education*, 1693) which used terms such as 'predominant passions' and 'prevailing inclinations' to introduce the topic of individual differences. Biggs and Telfer speak of differences in many areas, including types of ability (such as verbal, mathematical, spatial), preferences for processing information (convergent and divergent thinking), preferences for interacting with others, and so on.

Learning styles are sometimes listed as alternatives, such as:

Impulsive	versus	reflective
Analytical	versus	holistic
Passive	versus	active
Discovery	versus	imitation-oriented
Tactile	versus	auditory/kinaesthetic/visual

One starting point for workshop planners could be to do some reading about learning styles and learning strategies. Over the years these have been given separate emphases in teacher training courses, with varying degrees of clarity, but Hattie (2009: 195) speaks of 'the confusion of learning styles with learning strategies'. He summarises some of the styles that have been highlighted as: auditory, visual, tactile and kinaesthetic. A strategy, by contrast, is seen as something a learner chooses to use as a means of learning, rather than something which is an enduring characteristic of that person. Thus, in studies of language learners' strategies, the following processes have been identified (Cohen and Macaro, 2007: 11): clarification and verification, monitoring, memorisation, guessing/inductive inferencing, deductive reasoning, and practice.

Of course, none of us wants to be pigeon-holed for life, and in fact we may prefer one style for one type of learning and another for something different. To take a simple example, the case of the computer workshop participant quoted above illustrates a willingness to learn by tactile experimentation, but the same person might not have chosen that style to learn to ride a motorcycle. Still, it seems useful for a workshop presenter to be aware that in every group of people there is likely to be variety in the ways people want to learn, and incorporating a range of ways helps to cater for all. The following list is not a set of 'either/or' points. Rather, it is intended as a variety check for any workshop.

Three categories of learning style are often listed: auditory, visual, and kinaesthetic.

Visual learners enjoy learning by seeing. They are helped when something is shown. For them you can prepare charts, video and DVD clips, any kind of graphic. They can also be encouraged to summarise their own learning visually, such as through mind maps. They like to see a text even when you are explaining it orally.

For *auditory learners* listening is particularly important. They will enjoy songs, recorded interviews, a range of voices and even different accents. Asking individuals to read aloud from their group reports will also help this group.

Kinaesthetic learners enjoy sensations such as body movement and handling items. Try role-play, handling samples that illustrate the points being made, simulations, the use of cards that can be manipulated as they are grouped or sequenced, interviews with other participants, and so on. Changing places so as to work with different groups during the day can also help. Touching objects works especially well with topics that show people how to make things. Samples can be passed round for participants to examine them closely as they turn them round and look at details.

Learning skills, in contrast, are more specific than styles. Unlike learning styles, which some people believe are our life preferences, covering personalities, work preferences and so on, skills can be learned. Examples include creative skills, where workshop participants come up with original ideas, and processing skills, for example through completing worksheets by adding personal examples, reporting back in groups on short assigned readings, or responding to case studies (see the section on 'Workshop activities' on p. 93).

Another set of differences within any workshop will be the range of experience. By 'range' we mean not simply the amount, but rather, the type: experience as thinkers or doers, as supervisors or team-members, as innovators or improvers.

In summary, for workshop facilitators the challenge is not to identify which attenders might prefer to learn in which particular way, but to acknowledge that amongst any group of attenders there will be a kaleidoscope of differences and that these will be catered for by having a range of activities.

From the viewpoint of the workshop organiser, it is of little interest whether styles and strategies are fixed or flexible in an individual. What matters is that at any session there are likely to be people who learn in different ways, and in some cases are ready to be introduced to new ways of learning. As we shall see in the section on 'Workshop activities' (p. 93), there is an endless range of activities which can be used in workshops to fit all styles and strategies.

It is fair to say that the term 'learning styles' has come in for some criticism for being too rigid. For example, Hattie (2009: 197) concludes a review of many studies on this topic with the words 'Learning strategies, yes; enjoying learning, yes; learning styles, no.' He refers to researchers who doubt the ability of teachers (and we would include workshop facilitators) to work out what people's styles are in any way but random guessing. Our inclusion of information about learning styles in a book on workshops is not to suggest that presenters do a detailed analysis, but rather that they should be aware that there will be different learning preferences. Introducing variety in the presentation, processing and practising of new learning seems to make sense.

▶ Motivation

Although not all writers agree on a definition of the term, it is clear that individuals bring various types and degrees of motivation to a group activity such as a workshop (cf. Williams and Burden, 1997). Here are some aspects of motivation as they might apply to workshop participants.

Intrinsic and extrinsic motivation

The topic of motivation in learning has been analysed under many headings, often presented as binary choices. In the case of intrinsic and extrinsic motivation these could be summarised as the push and the pull factors. Motivation determines both the initial choice of whether or not to attend a workshop, as well as participation during the workshop. Let's describe these two types of motivation in terms of workshop attenders.

Intrinsic motivation starts with the choice to attend the workshop. Intrinsically motivated people have been driven to attend by a need or want of their own, as opposed to being sent there by an employer. There is something in the workshop title and/or description that might link with the person's own current interests or, alternatively, the title offers something that sparks curiosity, even though the person had not previously been interested in this topic.

Once the workshop starts, intrinsic motivation continues when participants see the activity as worthwhile in itself. The behaviour – taking part in, say, a case study discussion, a role-play or the analysis of a video clip – is 'performed for its own sake in order to experience pleasure and satisfaction' (Dörnyei, 2001: 27).

Extrinsic motivation, by contrast, refers to something that comes from without, going beyond a person's current interests. Perhaps someone signed up for a workshop for reasons outside the event, such as a suggestion by a supervisor. People might attend a workshop because they get a day off work to go to some interesting location or because it leads to a certificate which will help in their promotion.

While workshop organisers can't change the fact that some participants are not there voluntarily, it is often possible to 'win the person over' as some of our suggestions will show.

Descriptions of the workshop content in titles and publicity can cover both these types of motivation, since many attenders have mixed motives for participating. They may be glad to be out of the office for a day but also be genuinely curious about the topic.

The location of the workshop can be a draw for some people. Although it may not be the presenter's role to choose the location, it may be worth mentioning in the publicity any feature that might make it seem appealing. This could be the physical surroundings:

'… held in the peaceful surroundings of …'

Or it could be the opportunity it gives for practical work:

'The workshop will be held in the recently built buildings associated with the … Institute.'

Or even:

'If you arrive early, enjoy a coffee and muffins at the continental cafe next door.'

Another part of the extrinsic motivation could be that the workshop leads to some formal recognition.

'Workshop attenders will receive a certificate recognised by ...'

Integrative and instrumental motivation

Another distinction sometimes made is between integrative and instrumental motivation.

Integrative motivation applies to people attending a workshop in order to be part of (integrate with) the community. Perhaps others attending are part of an important unit at their place of work, or perhaps attending is seen as a 'rite of passage' amongst a particular group. This aspect of motivation is built on during the workshop through providing opportunities for group interaction, including food and coffee breaks long enough for talking to one another.

In fact, *group motivation* has recently been added to the influences on learning. Dörnyei (2001: 38) talks about a framework of interrelated group characteristics. These include the group's structure, the group's developmental level (cohesiveness, independence and productivity), and leadership style and behaviour. Although workshop groups do not have a permanent structure, since attenders usually come together simply for the event, the facilitator's role can have an influence, as examples will show.

Application for presenters

Integrative motivation can be supported if the workshop publicity includes quotes from previous attenders with whom potential attenders would identify. It can also help if the publicity mentions the 'team' aspect:

'Make up a group to take advantage of our group discount.'

'Last year this workshop was attended by ... from ... [your industry]'

Instrumental motivation 'describes a group of factors concerned with motivation arising from external goals' (Williams and Burden, 1997: 116). In relation to this aspect of motivation facilitators might, for example, negotiate beforehand the handing out of certificates of attendance.

Application for presenters

In addition to the suggestions above, instrumental motivation can be assisted in ways such as:

Sending in a report for an in-house journal
Naming the attenders
Highlighting some achievements of past attenders
Career reasons, including pay rises
'Freebies' associated with the workshop, such as industry-sponsored gifts, or a magazine subscription for the first twenty to enrol.

Finally, *cross-cultural aspects of motivation* come into play when the facilitator belongs to a different cultural group from the participants. Dörnyei (2001) illustrates this aspect with the concepts of individualism and collectivism. Some groups may be motivated more by individual achievement, while others may value group achievement more. Facilitators working with mixed groups find that one solution is to provide a mixture of activities, some based on individual and others on group achievement.

Demotivation

There is, of course, such a thing as demotivation, but this usually comes into play once the workshop has started. It can happen as a result of a range of causes, including participants feeling they have been made to look silly in front of others or, less personally, when the content or process is boring.

Application to presenters

Some types of demotivation can be predicted. Avoid the phenomenon of someone feeling foolish in front of their peers, by calling for volunteers when it comes to feedback time, rather than nominating people who may or may not want to stand in front of the room.

Another way to be alert for demotivation is to look for negative signs when people form groups and start talking amongst themselves. This is one reason not to spend all the group time preparing for your next input. Keep moving round the room, taking the emotional temperature, so to speak.

The workshop tasks: how motivating?

So far we have shown how the topic and its relationship to the attender might underline positive or negative aspects of motivation. One other aspect of workshops can affect motivation, namely the tasks that participants are asked to carry out. In the section on 'Workshop activities' (p. 93), we include suggestions for making these tasks as motivating as possible.

So far we have made some generalisations about attending to motivational aspects of learning during a workshop. We turn now to some more specific examples.

QUESTION

'When I was a primary school teacher I was very conscious that it was up to me to motivate the children. Now that I am running workshops for teachers I'm wondering whether that load shouldn't be more evenly shared with the adult participants. What do other facilitators feel? Am I really the one fully responsible for motivating these teachers?'

---

1   Choosing workshop topics

Topics that do not interest the participants are unlikely to be motivating. A good strategy is to find out as much as you can about your participants beforehand and to negotiate topics with the sponsors or the institution offering the workshop. At this point there is a chance to ensure the content suits all three stakeholders: the presenter, the sponsors and the participants. The following examples from facilitators show why this could be important:

▶ 'One organiser sent a list of three topics I was to cover in three hours. I could see immediately that we'd be breaking the speed barrier if we attempted all the suggestions, and that participants would end up with head knowledge but no chance to digest the new ideas. We had a series of email exchanges to ensure that all parties were happy.'

▶ 'I am sometimes asked to conduct workshops on topics I know little about. For my own sense of professionalism I feel obliged to say no. It's not that the topic is unsuitable, more that I'm not the right person for the topic.'

▶ 'From one negative experience, I realised that doing a two-day workshop by myself again would not be a good idea. For one thing, the teachers needed the support of at least two presenters to interact with them as they prepared materials for peer teaching.'

2   Offer choices during the workshop

If participants are offered a degree of choice, they can focus on those areas of teaching that are most relevant to them or cover them in the way they find most interesting. During the workshop the negotiation is about aspects such as:

Role-play a conversation
Work in groups of five, with three talkers and two observers.

The talkers
Choose one of these scenarios.

> friends meet at a bus stop
> dinner guests are waiting for the last person to arrive before eating
> three strangers find themselves at the same airport coffee table

The observer's instructions

Notes to the observers
Notice how they ...

make small talk	get a turn to speak
keep a topic going	change the topic
react to silence	

Figure 1.2 Example of a workshop activity

> The choice between two or more ways of doing an activity
> The relative time to be spent on each topic
> The time to be spent on spontaneous questions from participants.

Figure 1.2 is an example of an activity from a workshop on communication strategies that offers some choice in how participants complete a role-play.

Before starting, the facilitator who planned this activity asked: 'Would you rather all have a go at this in groups of threes, or would you like to have two people at the front as the rest of you observe?' With different workshops there will be different responses, sometimes depending on factors such as the time of day. After a heavy lunch some participants prefer to be passive. The content is identical in both cases, but what has changed is the participants' commitment to the activity because they have been given some choice.

3 Make explicit links with participants' concerns
It is not necessarily the case that participants with external or instrumental motivation will not join in or learn from a workshop, but it does mean that

the facilitator's approach may have to be slightly different. It may be necessary to show how the workshop content is linked to the participants' goals. For example, if the topic is one of the requirements for obtaining a teaching certificate, then make explicit exactly how the topic is one step on the way to getting the qualification.

Sometimes the facilitator can be creative, as in the case where one of us was teaching a group of secondary school teachers on the use of technology in the classroom. Their initial reluctance diminished somewhat when they were shown the results of a study that showed that teachers with such experience demonstrably find jobs more quickly and earn more than those who do not.

► Affect

The two main ways of finding out about the affective responses of workshop attenders seem to be by observation (during the session) and by self-reporting later. What we do know is that if people are not emotionally engaged, then other learning is unlikely to happen. For suggestions on dealing with inattention and boredom, see the section on 'Motivation' (p. 24).

The role of affect, or feelings, in the learning process is an important element in any plan for adult learning such as, in our case, workshops. The way people feel about what they are hearing plays a part in what happens to the new learning later, whether those feelings are negative or positive.

Pre-workshop planning

Including affect in workshop objectives

Traditionally, as we saw in the section on 'Setting goals' (p. 76), people in many professions write statements expressing what should happen for people by the end of a training event. These learning objectives (or outcomes) can refer to three aspects of the learning process. In the case of workshops, these objectives can say:

► What the attenders should know by the end, that they didn't know beforehand.
► What they should be able to do when the workshop finishes.
► What attitudes they should have towards the workshop content.

It is this third, attitudinal, aspect that we are concerned with in this chapter.

Wording outcomes

The wording of outcomes relating to people's feelings is often said to be the most difficult of the three categories, particularly when we have in mind that outcomes are meant to be measurable. A short quiz can test knowledge; participant demonstrations are a sign that skills have been learned; but how do we measure feelings?

A glance at sample outcomes shows some common words and phrases that are used for affective outcomes.

Workshop attenders should/will ...
> develop an appreciation of ...
> value the use of safe practices in ...
> appreciate the underlying purpose of ...
> feel competent to ...
> gain confidence in ...

It is one thing to have the head knowledge for a topic and even to demonstrate in a sheltered workshop environment how to do it. Back in the workplace, though, other factors may come into play, as the following vignette shows.

VIGNETTE

'I once attended a workshop for building apprentices on the topic of safety regulations on building sites. The organiser was a senior builder whose years in the trade had brought wisdom. He asked the participants a question.

"On the building site, who do you think gets appointed to be the safety officer?"

The apprentices came up with a number of suggestions: The senior person? The one with the fewest other responsibilities? Someone who's good at first aid?

All these answers turned out to be wrong.

"No. They'll appoint you as soon as you start your first job."

"Why us? We know less than everyone else."

"True. Also you have no authority. They'll appoint you because when you say 'Don't forget your safety helmet and the rope' they can just ignore you."

He had all their attention as he went on to present a session on safety, through role-plays and plenty of humour.'

In this case the presenter took into account realistic barriers to safety in the workplace even when everyone had the head knowledge of the rules, and the practical skills to use safety ropes and harnesses. As we'll see in Part 2, role-play can be a powerful learning tool.

Measuring outcomes

How might outcomes be measured at the end of a workshop? One common way is by self-reporting. Participants can be asked to grade their 'appreciation of / competence in / confidence about' on a before and after scale. Less formally, a small workshop can conclude with each participant saying briefly in what ways they have changed their attitudes to something in the course of a workshop.

Another way is to postpone the feedback from participants until there has been time for these qualities to develop back at the workplace. It may even be that the measurement comes from supervisors who did not attend the workshop themselves, but who see the difference it has made to the participants.

Negative affect during workshop activities

Once the workshop starts, the affective aspects of learning start to show, particularly when participants are asked to work in pairs or groups to do tasks. The first step is to recognise people's feelings.

Recognising negative affect

Recognising problems may be the first step in overcoming them. Here are some examples of negative affect that we have encountered in workshops. Although we have separated them, many of these overlap.

Anxiety
Participants worry that their weaknesses will be exposed in front of others.

Fear
Workshop participants fear they will be evaluated in some public way such as being issued certificates with grades.

Stress
Workshops held at awkward times bring stress. One example is that having to attend during school holidays brings a particular stress for parents whose children are out of school at the same time.

Anger

Understandably there can be resentment if the workshop is compulsory for employees who are seen as not measuring up in their workplaces. A workshop filled with the weakest staff members can be difficult to motivate.

Although the facilitator cannot change all these factors, the above is a summary of hints, from our experience, for dealing with them. More detailed suggestions follow.

We look next at presenters' concerns about negative feelings during workshops. Following each concern, we have some suggestions.

The irritator

QUESTION

'Something I have noticed in workshops is that one or more people (often just one) can start to irritate others. These are adults, not children. How can I deal with the situation without seeming bossy?'

It is true that some people can quite easily irritate others, including the presenter. Here are some behaviours we have noticed as irritants in workshops we have been part of.

► Dominating group activities by speaking first or over the top of others.
► Being occupied with other things, one of the most dramatic being not just answering a mobile phone, but actually proceeding to have a conversation on it in a loud voice.
► Constantly correcting or adding to the presenter's comments.
► Arriving late and asking for a re-run of the introduction.
► Whispering to another person all the time you are talking.

Since we are talking about affect, let's start with a suggestion about your attitude as the presenter. If possible, don't allow yourself to be personally offended by the behaviour. Rather, remind yourself that the presenter's role is to allow learning to happen for all the participants, and that your focus needs to be on the fact that this person is irritating them more than you.

A second suggestion relates to what action you might take. Have a graded list of solutions.

1   Ignore the problem
    If something happens once only or just for a short time, then dealing with
    it could make the atmosphere worse, not better. You can also ignore the
    problem even if it continues, provided it doesn't bother others. This can
    apply to checking and sending text messages.
2   Take an indirect approach
    If the problem continues, try walking closer to the whisperer or talker or
    phone-answerer and engaging them with eye-contact. This often draws
    the person's attention to the fact that you have noticed some behaviour
    that doesn't quite fit the rest of the workshop activity.
3   Give an impression of cooperation
    This is difficult if you don't feel cooperative, as in the case of the latecomer
    who wants a re-run of the early content.
       'I could go over it with you at lunch time if you want to sit with me.'
       'Do you have a colleague here who could bring you up to date at
    morning tea time?'
    Cooperation with the interrupter can have a positive effect on others.
       'You might be right on that point. You've given us an exception to the
    general point. Would anyone else like to give an example of an exception?'
4   Use body language
    For the participant who tries to cut in when you are talking, do the oppo-
    site of Suggestion 2 about eye contact. Turn away to jot something on the
    board, or stroll around the room looking at other people as if you haven't
    heard the interruption.
5   Invite others to make suggestions
    When one person is dominating a group, you can ask people whether
    they'd like to change groups after the break or not.
6   Direct action
    Finally there is the action that a person can't ignore.
       'I notice that you have had a lot of experience in this field. Am I right?
    It won't offend me if you decide there's nothing new for you here.' [In
    other words, 'Goodbye'.]

Nervous participants

QUESTION

'How can I respond to the situation where workshop participants seem very
nervous and afraid of participating?'

Table 1.2 Overcoming problems

Problem	Suggestion
Fear of looking inadequate	Announce early on in the workshop that any 'upfront' practice will be voluntary and that most of the practice teaching will be in small groups.
Fear of evaluation	Negotiate beforehand the idea of a 'certificate of attendance', not an assessment grade following the workshop.
Workshop held at an awkward time	Some problems can be predicted. It may be better to say no to running a workshop that starts immediately after school on Friday and runs all day Saturday and Sunday. Negotiate more friendly hours.
Compulsory attendance	Include in the workshop, suggestions that are within the capabilities of the group.
Not seeing the point of a particular activity	Explain why, as well as how, each activity is to be done.
Language limitations when people are using a second language	Invite people to report in pairs and then ask one of a pair to report what the other has said.

Nervousness is only one of the many feelings that can make a difference, for better or for worse, to a workshop. Earl W. Stevick (quoting Dulay, Burt and Krashen, 1982; in Arnold, 1999: 44) says that 'one's "affect" toward a particular thing or action or situation or experience is how that [situation] ... fits in with one's needs or purposes, and its resulting effect on one's emotions'. In workshops, affect can enhance or detract from teachers' attention.

The way people *think* about a workshop (before they arrive, during their attendance and on later reflection) usually parallels the way they *feel* about it. Thinking and feeling are interwoven, or, as Jane Arnold and H. Douglas Brown express it, 'the affective side of learning is not in opposition to the cognitive side' (Arnold, 1999: 1). Workshop facilitators, like classroom teachers, want to make learning more effective as they look for ways to 'overcome problems created by negative emotions and ... create and use more positive, facilitative emotions' (ibid., p. 2).

Overcoming learner helplessness

QUESTION

'What if participants say, "Nice ideas but they wouldn't let me do anything like this back at the office"?'

Another negative aspect of affect in workshops can be that some people have learned to see themselves as helpless when it comes to making a change. They may even feel that they have been sent to the workshop for negative reasons, as some of these comments from participants at one workshop show.

> 'They only sent me here to get me out of the way for a day. I'm at the bottom of the rung and nothing I do or say makes much difference.'

> 'It was kind of them to pay for my enrolment but I think they're doing it so they have ammunition later for sacking me.'

> 'Don't expect me to learn much. I've always been hopeless at taking new ideas on board.'

> 'If you don't make things difficult for me then I won't for you. This is the third retraining they've sent me on in three years. I'll be retiring soon anyway.'

There's not much a workshop organiser can do about people's reasons for being there, or even about their own feelings, but fortunately in most groups there are enthusiastic people as well as those who feel helpless or negative. Making a difference to the latter group can happen in various ways, not all of them from the leader.

1 Group dynamics can help. If possible, have the more negative people scattered through other groups, where the enthusiasm of others can make a difference.
2 Include in your case studies examples of people from previous workshops who have learned something despite a negative start.
3 During group work, try for some short periods of one-on-one time with anyone who has expressed a negative attitude. Ask why they feel like this and what could make a difference.

Positive affect

Building on feelings of success

For some people the biggest incentive to transfer their new learning from the workshop to their work or lives later is doing well in the workshop. If the tasks you set are manageable but not too easy, new but not overwhelming, then people will thrive. Harmless competition can help. Set up 'teams' to do some of the practical exercises, such as persuading others of a viewpoint.

If the teams are varied enough, it should not be the same group who always wins. In a long workshop it could help to mix up the groups, say, between the morning and afternoon sessions, to avoid an unhealthy sense of competition.

Putting it all together

Finally, here is a summary of some suggestions we have had from others.

1 Explain reasons for activities

One situation which often brings complaints from workshop participants is if they are asked to do something without knowing why. Take an instruction like this from a language workshop on teaching vocabulary through reading:

> 'Here's a passage from yesterday's newspaper editorial. I've blanked out every fifth word and I want you to see if you can fill them in.'

As they start writing, the facilitator is at the front preparing the next stage in the workshop. This gives the participants the chance to mutter to one another.

> 'This would be far too difficult for my students.'

> 'That's right and the subject would be quite irrelevant to them.'

The problem is that the facilitator has failed to inform the group that they are trying this out to experience the activity from their own standpoint. It was never intended to be a passage they could take and use with their next class.

2 Create an unhurried atmosphere

Imagine that the facilitator starts by announcing that time is short and that there is no time to waste on introductions. Participants who already have a strong sense of how short the time is will start with a heightened sense of stress. More positively, the facilitator might say:

> 'Rather than doing introductions right this minute, soon we'll be having an activity where you'll start to know one another by reflecting on the various classrooms you come from.'

Similarly, having an overview of the day's programme on the board or on a Powerpoint[1] slide will help to give people an idea of what to expect. Highlighting the coffee and lunch breaks is a useful 'trick'!

---

1. We use 'Powerpoint' to refer to any presentation software, including Keynote, Prezi or alternatives.

3   Recognise the concerns of participants
Perhaps the workshop participants' minds are full of their classroom problems. In one workshop, the presenter started by asking the teachers to
mention some reasons why it was difficult for them to encourage students to
speak English in the language class (which was the workshop topic). On the
board they built up a list like this:

> *Easier to speak their own language*
> *Class too big to monitor*
> *Lack courage to try speaking*
> *Not part of our classroom tradition*

The facilitator wrote these on one side of the board, and made it clear that
the workshop would cover all these points. She then referred to the list each
time one of the topics came up so that teachers could see the connection
between their concerns and the workshop content.

4   Find out beforehand about cultural differences
Groups from different countries may prefer different ways of working. Find
out beforehand what to expect, for example by talking to a colleague who
has taught in that country. If no information is available, it is useful to build
some flexibility into your programme, such as by having two versions of
some of the activities (for instance, one involving more public participation
and the other more silent work). As the day progresses, you can adjust to
your audience.

As we have shown, taking people's feelings into account is important in both
the planning and process of workshops. It makes connections with motivation (as discussed on pp. 30–2), and makes a difference to the way we plan
the workshop activities (as set out on pp. 32–6).

▶ Learner autonomy

Why are some attenders passive?

One might think that the name 'workshop' suggested action and involvement. It can therefore come as a surprise to some presenters to find that
some people come with the attitude of 'Tell me what I need to know and I'll
write it down.' Or, even more passively, 'Give me a handout with all the
information and I'll read it later.' The cynical response could be, 'Sure. Give
me your email address and I'll forward you the whole content ahead of time.'

We know that a workshop resembles an equation with a formula like this:

$$\text{Presenter} + \text{attenders} + \text{tasks} = \text{learning}$$

We look now at ways of overcoming passivity or, more positively, of encouraging autonomy.

What motivates attenders?

Here, in the imagined words of a workshop attender, are some attitudes that lead to a person being an active, and eventually autonomous, attender and learner.

1 'What I am learning is useful to me.'
   The challenge for someone preparing a workshop is to know enough about those who will be attending to make sure the content is useful. Here are some questions to ask beforehand.

   What is the range of experience in the group?
   Have any people mentioned problems on their applications?
   How many workshops have people already attended on this topic?

2 'I find I am usually successful in my work and that success increases my self-esteem.'
   In setting tasks for the workshop, consider balancing the manageable with the challenging. If everything is completely manageable in too short a time, then nothing new has been learned. On the other hand, if it takes too long to complete the tasks, the opposite can happen and some people will simply give up.
   As people are working on the tasks, keep moving round the room to note progress. Some may have reached a barrier, which they can be helped over. Perhaps you realise that for the next task, you need to demonstrate one step first, or perhaps give an example or two.

3 'The acceptance of other people in my efforts is important to me.'
   Other people can include fellow attenders as well as the presenter. Offering praise can help, provided it is realistic and genuine. See the section on 'Categorising and selecting activities' (p. 82) for more on organising tasks.

4 'The activities are fun and interesting.'
   You will build up a repertoire of successful activities, thinking in particular of successes and failures from the workshops you have already conducted.

Table 1.3 Offering choice

Suggestion	Helps learners by
Offer two or three activities for each practice time. Each should be labelled for its degree of difficulty.	Allowing them to choose their own level of difficulty.
Provide a list of all the activities. Set the activities out on separate tables round the room.	Allowing choice. There could be different activities to make a particular point. People refer to the list and select which they would like to do.
Have samples of the finished product available.	Showing the goal or objective.
When groups are looking at samples that have problems, indicate where they can find an analysis of the problem once they have tried to work it out for themselves.	Not making them wait for the leader/ presenter to give the 'answer'.

Choose resources that promote independence

The following features promote learner autonomy (adapted from Reinders and Lewis, 2008). The examples are for a practical topic.

Offer choice

Offering participants choice is a good way of differentiating content for different participants. Learners can be given different options in terms of:

> Content: for example, participants can be given different topics or scenarios and be asked to prioritise them.
> Method: a choice of different types of activities. These preferred activities could be used with the whole group, or individual participants could work with different tasks, or in different groupings (e.g., in a group of 20, you might have 3 pairs, 4 people working independently and two small groups of 5).
> Timing: this can be in terms of what to cover first, but can also refer to the amount of time to allocate per topic.
> Level: even if participants agree on the prioritisation of the topics, they may have different levels. You could group them on the basis of their experience.

Encourage self-directed learning

Not all learners have experience with directing their own learning. Workshops can be a good opportunity to develop the necessary skills, as

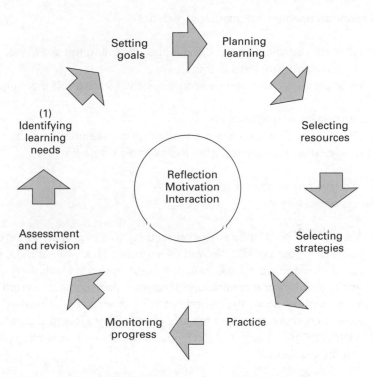

Figure 1.3 The independent learning process

participants can get help from you and from their peers. It is helpful, especially with longer workshops, to make the different steps of the self-directed learning process explicit. The diagram above is taken from Reinders (2010) and starts from a process of reflection; learners' motivation to engage in the learning process; and interaction with resources, other learners, and so on. For workshop facilitators it is useful to ask to what extent your participants have experience with each of these steps. For example, do they know how to 'identify their learning needs' (the first stage), and if not, how could they be helped to do this? Similarly, do they know how to set their own goals, plan their learning activities, select the most appropriate resources, select learning strategies, find opportunities for (controlled) practice, monitor their learning, and assess themselves?

Self-evaluation

For practical workshops, learners can be more autonomous if they are shown how to self-evaluate. (See Petty, 2004: 352–3.) This can happen in some of the following ways.

1 Respond to open-ended questions, such as:

> What are you finding most difficult about learning this skill?
> What are your strengths in this area?
> What problems have you overcome since we started this morning?

2 Use a checklist or questionnaire
Some practical skills lend themselves to being measured by a checklist which describes the features, as in the example on pages 43–7.

3 People give one another feedback
Here is one example.

> 'We were at a workshop where one activity was to prepare a poster as publicity for our project. We worked in groups for a while and then we put our posters up on the wall. The tutor placed a blank sheet on a small table in front of each one. Everyone had to move around the room, writing down their impressions of other people's posters. We were encouraged to write a mixture of specific praise and suggestions. Then each group collected the feedback sheets and sat down to read and discuss them.'

4 Measure the item beside a model
This can apply to skills such as:

> ▶ Using a new computer program to complete something.
> ▶ Making a craft object.

5 See if it works
Some products can be measured by whether they work or not, such as a survey that one group decided on, which could be tried out with another.

In all of these suggestions the self-critical skills being developed prepare someone for a workplace where there is not constant supervision. Participants learn:

> *Why* something is wrong
> *How* to correct faults.

They are not constantly waiting for a supervisor to come and tell them whether or not they have done well.

Is your teaching teacher- or student-directed?

Part 1

(0 = never, 1 = almost never, 2 = sometimes, 3 = almost always, 4 = always)

1 I learn what my students like, so I can make decisions based on their preferences.	
2 My students make their own plans to meet their goals.	
3 I learn what students can do, so that I can make decisions based on their abilities.	
4 My students monitor their results by comparing them with goals in order to determine whether their plans are working.	
5 There are instructional opportunities for students to set goals for what they want to learn and what they want to do.	
6 I set goals for students based on what they need or want, and what they are able to do to satisfy those needs and wants.	
7 There are instructional opportunities for students to adjust their plans frequently and repeatedly in order to improve their results.	
8 I make plans for how students will meet learning goals.	
9 My students learn by adjusting to their results until they know what choices and actions produce the results they want.	
10 I learn about my students by adjusting to results repeatedly until I know what decisions and actions produce the results I want for them.	
11 I have frequent opportunities to set goals for what students need and want to learn.	
12 There are instructional opportunities for students to discover for themselves what they like, what they want, and what they can do to satisfy their interests and needs.	
13 My students use their evaluations of results to adjust their plans in order to improve next time.	

14 I monitor students' results by comparing them with their goals in order to determine whether my plans are working for them.	
15 There are instructional opportunities for students to construct plans to meet their learning goals.	
16 My students learn to set goals based on what they need or want, and what they're able to do to satisfy their needs and wants.	
17 There are instructional opportunities for me to follow through on constructing plans for students to meet their learning goals.	
18 My students learn what they like, so they can make choices based on that knowledge.	
19 I use my evaluations of student results to adjust their goals, plans, and actions so that they will improve next time.	
20 There are instructional opportunities for me to construct plans for students to meet their learning goals.	
21 There are instructional opportunities for students to act independently on their plans to meet their learning goals.	
22 There are instructional opportunities for me to discover what students like, what they want, and what they can do to satisfy their interests and needs.	
23 My students learn what they can do, so they can make choices based on their abilities.	
24 There are instructional opportunities for me to adjust plans frequently and repeatedly in order to improve the results.	

Adapted from: Mithaug, D. et al. (2007). *Self-instruction Pedagogy. How to Teach Self-determined Learning.* Springfield, IL: Charles C. Thomas.

CHECK YOUR SCORE USING THE SUGGESTED ANSWERS IN PART 2.

Part 1 Write down your rating for each question from part 1, add up the total and divide by 12.

Teacher-directedness		Student-directedness	
1 I learn what my students like, so I can make decisions based on their preferences.		7 There are instructional opportunities for students to adjust their plans frequently and repeatedly in order to improve their results.	
3 I learn what students can do, so that I can make decisions based on their abilities.		21 There are instructional opportunities for students to act independently on their plans to meet their learning goals.	
6 I set goals for students based on what they need or want, and what they are able to do to satisfy those needs and wants.		15 There are instructional opportunities for students to construct plans to meet their learning goals.	
8 I make plans for how students will meet learning goals.		4 My students monitor their results by comparing them with goals in order to determine whether their plans are working.	
10 I learn about my students by adjusting to results repeatedly until I know what decisions and actions produce the results I want for them.		12 There are instructional opportunities for students to discover for themselves what they like, what they want, and what they can do to satisfy their interests and needs.	

Teacher-directedness		Student-directedness	
11 I have frequent opportunities to set goals for what students need and want to learn.		9 My students learn by adjusting to their results until they know what choices and actions produce the results they want.	
14 I monitor students' results by comparing them with their goals in order to determine whether my plants are working for them.		2 My students make their own plans to meet their goals.	
17 There are instructional opportunities for me to follow through on constructing plans for students to meet their learning goals.		23 My students learn what they can do so they can make choices based on their abilities.	
19 I use my evaluations of student results to adjust their goals, plans, and actions so that they will improve next time.		5 There are instructional opportunities for students to set goals for what they want to learn and what they want to do.	
20 There are instructional opportunities for me to construct plans for students to meet their learning goals.		16 My students learn to set goals based on what they need or want, and what they're able to do to satisfy their needs and wants.	
22 There are instructional opportunities for me to discover what students like, what they want, and what they can do to satisfy their interests and needs.		13 My students use their evaluations of results to adjust their plans in order to improve next time.	

Teacher-directedness		Student-directedness	
24 There are instructional opportunities for me to adjust plans frequently and repeatedly in order to improve the results.		18 I students learn what they like, so they can make choices based on that knowledge.	
Total score		**Total score**	

Adapted from: Mithaug, D. et al. (2007). *Self-instruction Pedagogy. How to Teach Self-determined Learning.* Springfield, IL: Charles C. Thomas.

▶ Memory

Workshops are usually short interludes in people's working lives, but their effects are intended to spread over the next months. That can happen, of course, only if people remember the new ideas they have met. Much of what we read about memory in the general literature is a response to occasions when memory doesn't work. In this section we consider what is known about memory in the learning process. We then apply those principles to the planning of workshops.

From short-term to long-term memory

It is said that 'the process of remembering involves information passing from our short-term memory into our long-term memory' (Petty, 2004: 1). In order to move from the 'forgetting category', of information which is carried briefly in the brain before being lost, new learning needs to be processed in ways that make sense to the learner.

One response to this theory is that people can leave a workshop with something that helps later as a memory jogger. This could be in one or more of these forms.

1 Handout summaries can be helpful, particularly if the participant has had a part in completing it. 'Close' paragraphs are an example. Towards the end of the workshop people can be invited to complete a summary statement like this:

> 'During the workshop we examined ... techniques for quilting.
> One technique I'd like to try out soon is ....
> This involves ....'

2 Another type of summary is the labelled diagram. Again, if the participants complete the labels themselves, remembering will be helped. The
   labels could be added in a list at the foot of the diagram but not in the
   right order.

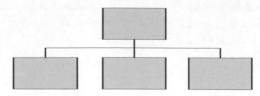

Or indicate causality/order

The section on 'Categorising and selecting activities' in Part 2 has practical ideas about tasks to plan for the workshop which help participants to
process the new ideas.

Speed of delivery

Another factor in remembering new information is the speed at which it is
presented. Learning has to happen at a pace that is digestible: not so slowly
that the process is boring but not so fast that the details are lost.

   Some workshop presenters whose natural delivery is quite fast, need to
practise one of these techniques:

▶ Pause briefly after important statements.
▶ Repeat information using different words or examples.
▶ Emphasise key terms in a sentence.

For more on this topic, see page 190.

Spaced learning

Ideally, learning that takes place in chunks, with time in between, is more
memorable than when the same amount of time spent learning, but in one
big chunk. The trouble about workshops is that they usually occur in blocks

of time. Repeating the same thing, even in different ways, may seem like a waste of that time.

Here are some ideas for practising the principle of spaced learning.

▶ Follow-up assignments can help, although they are more work for the presenter.
▶ Participants can take away ideas for practising or applying new ideas themselves later.
▶ After coffee or lunch breaks, start the next session with a quick review activity.

Relevance

Information is more likely to be stored long-term if it seems relevant to the listener the first time it is heard. The challenge for a workshop presenter is often trying to make material relevant to a very diverse group of people.

Meaningfulness can come in various ways during a workshop. One obvious way is to keep your illustrations current. You don't want people who have attended your workshops in the past to be asking, 'Did she tell that joke about ...?'

One source of illustrative examples is the audience. After listing some general principles, give people a couple of minutes to note down answers to the question, 'When could this be important in your context?' Hearing other people's examples is a helpful way of seeing the relevance of a new idea.

Retrieval

So far we have talked about making sure that the new learning is stored in the long-term memory. Now we turn to the topic of retrieval. How does the workshop attender find that information later, at the right moment? Mnemonics have a long history in the retrieval process. Do you remember any mnemonics from your childhood? For example, was there a word you memorised as a way of recalling the colours of the rainbow? The first time I visited Canada, friends were surprised that I could recite the names of the Great Lakes. This relatively useless (to me) piece of information was lodged in my brain thanks to the acronym HOMES.

Adults as social learners

The social aspect of learning is an important contributor to success or failure in education and has received a lot of attention, especially in recent years, to the point where there is now talk of a 'social turn' (Block, 2003). This refers to a recognition of the fact that learners are not simply individual processors of information but instead are human beings, who bring previous experiences, feelings and motivations to the classroom. People are members of numerous social networks and these affect many aspects of their learning, from what they consider worthy of learning in the first place, to the support they get while learning. As a result, education now places much more emphasis on the social aspect of learning and the ways learners can learn with and from each other. Workshops are ideally suited for social learning, with their emphasis on learning by doing, and learning in pairs and groups. Below we look at some aspects of social learning that workshops can support.

▶ Collaborative learning

Collaborative activities are common not only to formal education but also to informal learning, such as in the workplace and in the home. In this section we will look at some of the pedagogical benefits of collaboration and look at its role in adult learning, with particular reference to workshops.

Collaboration is a powerful element in learning, in which learners work together, with or without guidance from a teacher. Collaboration has a number of learning benefits. Firstly, the shared knowledge of two or more people is greater than that of the individual. In other words, what could be impossible for one person to complete may be possible for a group (Slavin, 1990). For this reason, many workshops include activities where participants have to combine their experiences and knowledge. Secondly, collaboration requires active participation; learners cannot rely on the instructor but have to engage with other participants to complete a task or to create knowledge. Many workshop presenters alternate between teacher-led and collaborative tasks, to avoid passive attendance and to keep participants involved. Collaborative learning also requires learners to make their reasoning explicit, and to develop and revise their personal knowledge on the basis of new knowledge provided by other members of the group. This is a very active process, and one that involves the critical examining of one's own and others' ways of thinking. This type of exchange can lead to insights that may otherwise be difficult to accomplish if the only input comes from the workshop presenter.

In a study of collaborative learning in language education, Good and Brophy (1987) found that 26 out of 41 studies reported significantly greater learning in classes using collaborative methods; 14 of the remaining ones did not find significant differences and only one found a negative effect. This appears to indicate that collaborative learning can and often does have a positive impact on the learning process.

Not all learners like collaborative learning, however. Many workshop participants make comments on feedback forms like:

'I don't want to discuss things constantly with my neighbour. I came here to learn from an expert!'

'I have never enjoyed group work. I feel that only some people get to do most of the talking and I don't feel I learn a lot.'

We will deal with some of these criticisms in more detail in Part 3 of this book but it is clear that not all collaborative learning is successful. Slavin (1990) has identified a number of factors that need to be taken into account in planning collaborative activities. These include:

Identifying clear objectives
Encouraging personal responsibility
Assigning specialised tasks to individual members
Providing for ways of adopting the process and outcomes to individual needs
Providing equal opportunities.

In addition, the task needs to be sufficiently complex for group work to show more expertise than work from isolated individuals, and be multi-faceted so that each individual can make a valuable contribution.

If these conditions are met, many adults do in fact enjoy group and pair work. An important benefit in these cases is that the type of learning mirrors that which participants are likely to encounter in the workplace; it may model ways of working together and solving problems that will be helpful well after the workshop is over.

▶ Scaffolding

Two terms were coined by Lev Vygotsky in the first part of the 1900s, both of them relevant to workshop presenters. A *zone of proximal development*

(ZPD) 'is the difference between what a learner can do with and without help' (Banas and Velez-Solic, 2013: 11). In workshop terms this would refer in particular to performance outcomes/objectives which you would like participants to achieve by the end of the session. These could be practical skills, or affective achievements such as gaining in confidence. With support from you and their colleagues they could achieve these but without support they could not. The second term, *scaffolding*, as its literal origin suggests, is some temporary support needed until something more solid is in place. Scaffolding is the focus of this next section.

In the case of workshops, the support can come from the presenter and, through the presenter's organisation of activities, from other workshop attenders. Just as the literal scaffolding on a building is reduced when the structure is strong enough, so the support offered to participants is at first strong but gradually reduced as they gain knowledge, expertise and confidence.

What form might the support take? Banas and Velez-Solic list a number of suggestions for their work, with online support, which we can translate into workshop activities. Their first suggestion is that sometimes a problem needs to be shown one part at a time rather than all together. Of course this is not always the case. Sometimes it helps to see the 'big picture' before plunging into details, but other processes are learned better if they are introduced one by one. To change the scaffolding metaphor, picture the many cooking shows presented on television. Viewers see the cook add ingredients and perform actions one by one until the dish is finally ready. In your subject area you will no doubt think of topics other than building or cooking that require step-by-step learning.

Their second suggestion is 'removing extraneous or distracting factors' (2013: 12). In a workshop this can mean going to a clear area where equipment is not mixed up with books, notes and bags. It goes without saying that mobile phones ringing in the middle of a workshop come under the heading of distractions.

Then there is the suggestion to ask guiding questions. This is part of the process of discovery learning, which is covered in more detail in the section on 'Giving focus to discussions' (p. 102). The questions may include some requiring simple yes/no answers but they go on to higher levels which guide people to think for themselves about what they are being shown.

Regular feedback is another important part of scaffolding and includes commendations as well as suggestions. In a recent workshop that one of us was organising, the participants needed to practise introducing their specialty to others. At the end of each short speech the audience were invited to give these two types of feedback. At first they would only praise one another because they were so anxious to boost the confidence of nervous speakers, but eventually they agreed that making one, more critical, constructive suggestion to each person would lead them all to see ways of improving. Finally they recommend modelling the end results. The presenter herself makes a short speech introducing a topic new to the participants, before asking them to take a turn. At other times the 'model' might be a finished product which needs to be prepared beforehand.

By following these and related suggestions, the workshop presenter will finally be able to remove the 'scaffolding' and send participants on their way better prepared for independence.

Adults as experiential learners

While most people in the twenty-first century would agree that children learn through experiences, not everyone takes into account the role that experience plays in adult learning. If there was no need to experience new topics, then attending workshops would lose its point. Why not simply read a book or listen to a recorded talk on the topic of choice? Before we move to the applications of experiential learning for workshop presenters, we look at what is known of the role of experience in learning.

Defining experience

The word 'experience' is not particular to education. Various general dictionaries define it in words like these:

Direct personal participation
Observation
Contact
Personal involvement
Doing, seeing or feeling.

These general descriptors need to be examined more closely when it comes to learning experiences. It is possible to be somewhere, to see something happening, and even occasionally to do something ourselves and yet not to have learned anything. Think about this person's experience.

'By mistake I went into the wrong room at a meeting place and found myself listening to a talk about physics. That's a topic I know nothing about and, dare I admit, have not the slightest interest in. The speaker was lively, interesting, and engaged his audience through his illustrations and demonstrations. At the end he said, "Let's have a quick quiz on what we've just been seeing."

We all noted our answers to the questions and, to my amazement, I had a 100% score. When I thought about that later, this seemed to be the explanation. His questions related to theory, which he explained well. They did not relate to the wider context of his topic (I had no idea what that was) or to its applications (I certainly couldn't have used the information for anything). In other words, my results reflected good teaching, not good learning. Furthermore, a week later I had forgotten everything.'

Expressed another way, head knowledge is not the same as experiential knowledge. Experiencing new learning in ways that lead to lasting learning requires a number of features which we look at now.

Concentration

To experience something new, the learner needs to concentrate on what is happening. We may be able to do something automatically, as do animals who are taught to respond in a certain way to specific commands, but that is not the same as thinking about the reasons and processes and outcomes of what we are doing.

People have different ways of concentrating. For some, background music is essential to relaxing enough to be able to learn. For others, any kind of background sound is a distraction, whether it is Tchaikovsky, the Beatles or a crying baby. These individual differences mean that workshop organisers don't have an easy time helping everyone to concentrate. However, some aspects of presentations can be guaranteed to hinder concentration: a boring, monotonous voice, lights that are too glaring, blurred images on a screen, can all make concentration difficult. Then there is the question of feeling hungry or thirsty. The water dispensers that are often provided in meeting rooms help with half of that problem.

However, concentration is not entirely up to another person; part of the ability to concentrate rests with the attender. As we saw in the section above on motivation, there needs to be a mental set that wants to attend to the learning experience, rather than simply going through the motions.

Making mistakes

Another feature of experiential learning is to learn from one's mistakes. Not all presenters appreciate the importance of this, as one workshop attender found in the early days of computers (see our first vignette, on page 21). Educators (and parents) know that making mistakes is not something to feel foolish about; rather it is something to learn from. Experiential learners ask themselves questions.

Why did that go wrong?
What would happen if I ...?
Let's try ...

Anxiety

Anxiety, and its opposite, feeling relaxed, are two factors that can affect experiential learning. For some people, being asked to try out new skills, especially under observation, can induce anxiety, and in turn lead to a poor performance. Like motivation and affect, which we considered earlier (pp. 24 and 30), anxiety can have both internal and external causes. The workshop presenter does his or her best to lower anxiety but some worrying can be a part of the personality rather than the fault of the workshop process.

Giftedness

A more controversial topic is giftedness. While some workshop presenters may start with the words, 'Anyone can learn to ... if they try', experience would suggest that some of us are likely to have a natural aptitude for one area of learning and others for a different area. People come to a workshop with different beliefs about their own giftedness:

'I've always been hopeless at ...'

'They tell me I'm quite good at ...'

'I may not be great at ... but I enjoy giving it a go.'

Some of these beliefs and fears may be well founded, whereas others may have become what is sometimes called a self-fulfilling prophecy.

In summary, if you are running a workshop on public speaking, then part of the participants' experience must be to get up and speak. If the topic is learning about a new computer program, then part of the time must be spent actually using it. Other sections of Part 1 have more to say on this topic (see the section on 'Principles of adult learning', pp. 21–47). In the next section we turn to the role of the presenter in taking this theory into account.

The *experience* of learning in workshops

▶ The learner's contribution

So far we have talked about principles of adult learning, addressing these questions:

What do we know about the different ways people learn?
How can learners be motivated?
What place does affect play in the learning process?
To what extent can adult learners be autonomous?
What is the effect of learning with others?
How far can people be enabled to experience new ideas?

We now turn more specifically to the way adults actually experience learning when they are in workshops. We draw on a mixture of theory, as summarised above, and examples as they apply to learning in workshops rather than in traditional classrooms.

Although the words 'learner-centred teaching' have been used for some time, they usually apply to classroom learning, and often to young people. What contribution can learners make when they attend workshops in order to gain new knowledge and skills? One workshop attender gives a viewpoint.

'At a recent conference we were invited to choose from a range of sessions variously labelled talks, workshops and poster sessions. Nobody really explained to us what the difference was. By the end of the conference most of us were getting the idea by trial and error. Why don't they define things?'

This person has a valid point. What should people expect if they attend a workshop rather than a talk? The word 'work' gives a strong hint: in workshops the intention is that learners should contribute in various ways. The section 'Why workshops' (p. 13) spells out some of these in detail, but in summary, the learners' contributions can include any or all of the following:

Exchanging experiences with other participants
Meeting new ideas and skills, particularly by experiencing these in a variety of ways

Processing new ideas through reflective tasks
Practising skills
Planning ways to apply the new learning later.

We now see in more detail how the contributions might look.

Problem solving

Of course there are huge differences between the ways children and adults learn. For one thing, adults are adding new learning to a lifetime of knowledge and experience. There are, though, a number of parallels and one of these is that learning takes place as we solve problems for ourselves.

Think of this example. You are watching a small child try to do a jigsaw which someone has decided is age-appropriate. You notice that she is about to put the next piece in upside down. Which option do you choose: take it from her hand and demonstrate the right way, or let her work it out? Unless the child has reached the point of screaming with frustration, you let her work it out. Why? For the same reason as workshops set tasks that include problem solving. We learn by trial and error.

As with this childish example, the workshop presenter will have designed tasks, appropriate to the topic and the participants' experience, which lead to learning by doing. Of course, the leader is also alert for frustration. In a roomful of people, some will be more patient than others, some will learn faster than others. Knowing when to step in and make suggestions is something that comes by experience, and by asking, 'Would you like to keep trying or shall I give you a hint?'

Building on knowledge and experience

There is nothing more time-wasting than saying to a room full of people with mixed experience, 'Some of you know quite a bit about this topic and others are beginners, so for the sake of the beginners we'll start from scratch and pretend that nobody knows anything.' How does that feel for the people who came to take their knowledge to another level?

This attitude reflects a cartoon that appeared in an educational journal some time ago. A row of animals was waiting at the starting line of a running race: a snake, a kangaroo, a monkey, a bear, an eagle and others. The person in charge was saying, 'So as to be fair, we are all going to follow exactly the same rules.'

The workshop organiser tries to find out beforehand the range of experience within a group, but even if that information is not complete it's a fair guess that people will have different starting points. The tasks can be presented with options such as these:

▶ Form groups with mixed experience if people want to learn from one another.
▶ Offer choices of activity if people want to move at their own pace.
▶ Move around the room, monitoring that people are happy with the group they have chosen.
▶ Prepare instructions at different levels of complexity.

Knowing what you know

Part of the learning experience is being aware of what has been learned. There is such a thing as knowing something without realising it. Workshops can start with some activity that reminds people what they know already, through:

Self-administered quizzes
Structured interviews with others
Short performance tasks.

Then, from time to time during the workshop, they can be reminded of what they know and can do. Some of this happens informally as the presenter moves around the room giving individual feedback, but there are other ways too, such as these:

▶ Go round the circle asking people to say one new thing they have learned and one thing they would like to know more about.
▶ Ask some people to display samples of practical work while others wander round the room looking.

The final measure of what has been learned may or may not come at the end of the workshop. For some subjects, people will be aware of their knowledge only when they apply it later.

The social experience

For many people the social aspect of the learning experience will be the one they report on first when they return from the workshop. They will report on people they have met whose company they enjoyed and who encouraged them in their learning. They may even mention the names of people they plan to keep in touch with.

Ways of encouraging the social aspect of learning are mentioned from time to time in this book, but let's mention one here: food and drink breaks. These are not time-wasters to be cut short because 'We have a lot to get through.' They are a chance for people to exchange ideas about the day and, in some cases, to pass on hints about how to get the most from the workshop.

PART 2
Teaching in workshops

The *experience* of delivering workshops

For many, even highly qualified teachers, delivering workshops is a new and demanding experience. Especially initially, the experience can be fraught with challenges, but most presenters find that, over time, workshops become one of their favourite staff development activities. Below are the experiences of some workshop presenters, some positive, some less so, starting with a reflection from a teacher with many years of experience:

'During my professional life I've had the chance to teach classes, give lectures and run workshops. In my opinion, here's why workshops are the most satisfying experience of the three from the viewpoint of the person in charge.'

Table 2.1 summarises the differences and shows why, in my opinion, the experience of running a workshop is more satisfying than the other two modes. It is satisfying to be meeting people as an equal. True, the presenter does have knowledge and skills which participants are keen to learn about but the way in which these are imparted is more collegial than 'top-down'. When the presenter draws up a chair and joins the group, then it's clear that his or her role is not one of the distant expert.

Then there's the freedom to play around with the timing. Coffee breaks, for instance, are usually flexible (although it pays to check this one if caterers are involved) so it's possible to finish a few minutes earlier rather than later.

Table 2.1 Comparisons between delivery methods

	Class teaching	Lecturing	Workshop
Relationships	unequal	distant	equal
Focus of role	instructing	informing	facilitations
Length	dictated by others	dictated by others	flexible
Physical role	up-front	up-front	moving round
Time flow	fixed	fixed	in leader's hands
Resources	often designed by others	abstract sources	experientially based

VIGNETTE

'I still shudder, thinking back to that first workshop I did a few years ago. Seventy people turned up and were expecting me to entertain them for a full day. From the first moment it was clear to me this day was going to be different from any other before. My cheerful "Good morning, how is everybody doing?" was met with an eerie silence. Stony-faced, most of the participants would sit through the rest of the morning. My questions were met with blank stares and when I asked them to work in small groups, some just went and did something else. I think I counted the minutes until the first coffee break and quickly disappeared from the room to catch my breath. Oh, how I dreaded going back into the room! After lunch several of the participants did not return, and after the afternoon tea break we were down to about half our original number. My host explained that many had travelled from far and had to return home. I wasn't so sure. I don't know how I survived the rest of the day, but I did. Afterwards I vowed never to do a workshop again!

Over the years I have realised some of the things that went wrong. I guess one of my main mistakes was to assume that a workshop in one country was going to be similar to a workshop in another. Participants in this country simply had different expectations, needs, and wants from those of the participants I had taught before. Most of them probably expected more from me in terms of input and direction. Perhaps my workshop should have been more similar to a lecture, at least in the first hour or so, and perhaps I should have also included more and clearer instructions for the activities. I mistook their silence for a lack of willingness to cooperate, but perhaps it was anxiety about being asked to speak out and work in public. I could have started with some silent work or pair work rather than asking people to respond to questions in front of the whole room.

This experience has taught me about the importance of affect in workshops, both the participants' and my own. I now come better prepared and have become better at working out what it is participants expect, and tailor my workshops to that. I now also know that seventy participants is a lot for a workshop (as opposed to a lecture), and aim to limit the number to thirty-five when possible. I also find all-day workshops extremely exhausting, both for me and the participants, and now try to offer two half-day workshops instead when I can.'

Here is a more neutral experience from a teacher trainer from Auckland in New Zealand.

VIGNETTE

'What I found to be different is that you are facilitating a space where people actually do things, rather than listen to you, so you go in with tasks rather than things to say. The learning you plan is the task and what people do with it – rather than what you tell people – so your plan will look very different, with tasks which you hope are going to generate interest, engagement, learning and discussion, and options (contingency plans) based on what could happen. Some university lecturers are great at planning in this way and the experience of being a workshop participant is a very rich one. On the other hand, some lecturers, while they may be engaging speakers, are hopeless workshop facilitators, misunderstanding the fact that the process of doing the tasks is the learning. Instead they see tasks as tacked onto the input they give, with the result being that their workshop tasks feel empty and lack challenge.

In terms of the actual session, I find that the demands on the presenter are different too. Like a traditional lecture, you need to set the scene, engage the participants initially, outline where the session is heading and what you hope will be the outcomes. However, your added value in the session is down to how you set up each task and the transitions, how you support participants during tasks, and how you are able to respond afterwards to what participants do or say. That's the key difference – you expect and plan for far more involvement than in a traditional "speaker role" and so need to be far more responsive. You also need to be able to manage people in a way that makes them feel comfortable and prepared to contribute, take risks, learn actively and engage with the people around them to a far greater extent than if you are lecturing.'

Nick Moore, language teacher and teacher educator, Auckland

Critical incidents

A critical incident has been defined as 'an unplanned and unanticipated event that occurs during a lesson and that serves to trigger insights about some aspect of teaching and learning' (Richards and Farrell, 2005: 113). The critical-incident technique looks at key moments in a teacher's career or development that have had a major impact on their thinking, their beliefs, or their teaching practice (and, more often than not, all three). Critical incidents can be used as a reflective tool for teachers to become aware of their own values and experiences, and changes therein. Critical incidents usually teach us a lot about ourselves and can help us to understand why we teach in the way we do. Below, a number of teachers share some critical incidents in facilitating workshops and the impact they had.

'I am embarrassed to share the experience of one my first workshops, when a participant came to me during the break and said "you've been teaching us about the 'negotiated syllabus' [an approach to syllabus design that starts from a group discussion] but why haven't you used that with us?" That really brought home the old saying "practise what you preach".' (Cindy C., Poland)

And on a more positive note:

'The first time I really experienced the power of workshops was when a woman approached me after the workshop, almost tearful, saying how this had been the first time she felt she'd had a voice rather than having teachers talk at her.'

YOUR TURN

What are some of the 'critical incidents' in your own teaching (either in workshops or in class)? How have these helped you?

Bringing it all together: what makes a good facilitator?

From the above it is clear that there is a very wide range of experiences, and what may work in one context may not in the next. Nonetheless, it is possible to identify some key characteristics of workshop facilitators, both on the basis of previous studies and from facilitators' reflections. In summary form, successful facilitators:

Are flexible
Exude confidence
Encourage participation
Build on participants' knowledge
Are sensitive to participants' well-being
Clarify expectations
Help participants to link theory with practice
Encourage critical reflection
Control pace and direction
Enhance understanding
Give constructive feedback
Learn from their own mistakes.

Planning and organising workshops

In this section we pose, and suggest answers to, five questions which have helped workshop presenters in their planning. In summary, these relate to:

Goal setting
Time options
Balancing input from you and activity by attenders
Balancing serious and relaxed activity types
The difference between activities for different times.

What are the workshop goals?

This basic question needs to be sorted out with the organisers beforehand. For example, will participants be expected to gain something from the workshop which will be part of their promotion process? In this case there are two options. One is to develop some formal way of assessing the progress of individuals; the other is to issue an attendance certificate to everyone who attends.

For Option 1, be wary of volunteering to assess work samples following the workshop. Particularly in the case of people who are offering workshops in their own spare time, this can be a time-consuming task. Think twice before offering to grade tasks which could take hours to go through.

In the case of Option 2 the task should be simpler. People sign an attendance sheet and everyone who signs receives a certificate. Not too much can go wrong here, you might think. In our experience, human nature being what it is, if there are high stakes in receiving one of these certificates you may find that there are more signatures than there are people in the room. A simple head count can sometimes sort this out. On the other hand, the awarding of the certificate may not be your responsibility. If you are not required to sign the certificates, then ask the organisers to do the checking. You may also need to consider your policy on people who arrive late. Will someone who turns up half-way through the workshop still receive a certificate?

Apart from this formal assessment, it may be that the goals are more tangible, such as completing a piece of work for which no grade is given.

There is more on goal setting in the next section and more on assessment in the section on 'Feedback and assessment' (pp. 118–22).

How much time do you have and how much do you need?

One of the considerations as you plan your workshop will be the time available to you. 'Time' means actual time minus introductions, tea and coffee breaks, wind-ups, 'thank you' speeches and final presentations. Some workshop presenters are asked ahead of time how long they need for their topic, but as we know, most topics can be dealt with in any time-span from an hour to a week.

Even once you have been given the proposed time, be aware that the workshop attenders may have a looser understanding of the starting time than you. As we discuss elsewhere (p. 32), the affective aspects of the workshop will depend partly on how you deal with the fact that there are only half the intended audience there at the opening time. Negative comments such as, 'I see that time management is not one of the strengths of today's workshop attenders' will do nothing to enhance the atmosphere. Those who hear you don't want to be blamed for the non-arrival of others.

The balance between teacher input and participant activity

A workshop, as its name suggests, is a time when attenders expect to do some work. The question is, how much? Either extreme will annoy people:

1 The presenter turns the 'workshop' into a talk.
2 Participants receive no input of theory as the basis for tasks they have to complete.

As a rule of thumb, the proportion of time spent holding the floor should be balanced in favour of the participants and should be spread throughout the session.

The balance between serious and relaxed activity

This question is harder to quantify. What do we mean by serious? What is a relaxed activity? To use an analogy, a workshop is like a well made fruitcake. It needs enough solid ingredients to hold it together but enough fruit to make it deserve its name. Feedback from one workshop will give suggestions for the next. Think of including as one of your feedback questions:

What did you think of the balance of activity types?
Not enough fun / about the right balance / not enough content

Now and again each workshop presenter should go and attend an event organised by someone else. If the experience is a pleasant one, there will be plenty to imitate; if not, then learning by others' mistakes will make the event worthwhile.

The difference between pre-, in- and post-workshop activities

Finally, it is worth clarifying in your mind whether you want people to do activities before and after the actual workshop. Here are some suggestions.

Pre-workshop activities

Table 2.2 gives suggestions for activities and the benefits they will provide.

Table 2.2 Pre-workshop activities

What?	Why?
Samples of people's work	To inform you of their level As the basis of feedback from peers
Completed questionnaires	As an opening activity: results are combined to show patterns
Questions to be answered by the presenter	So that participants direct some of the content
Items to recommend (e.g. books)	For people to learn more from a display on tables as people move around taking notes

In-workshop activities

For suggestions here, see the section on 'Workshop activities' (p. 93).

Post-workshop activities

After the workshop is over, there are several options for follow-up activities. In summary, these involve three questions:

Who will see or give feedback on the activities?
What is the timeline for completing them?
What might the activities be?

Table 2.3 summarises some of the options in no particular order.

Table 2.3 Options for workshop activities

What	When?	Who?
On-task observation and feedback	As soon as possible after the workshop	Local supervisor or peer
A piece of work	Over several weeks	Workshop presenter if it can be sent by email
Report back online	A month or two later	All workshop attenders, perhaps using an online forum
Written report	As soon as possible	To be read by sponsors
Portfolio	For the follow-up workshop	All attenders plus presenter
Formal test	Determined by the professional body	An anonymous examiner

Workshop contexts

▶ Who attends?

In most workshops people have something in common. The link may be professional, or it may be the wish to learn the same new skill or to volunteer for the same role. Here are some specific groups who may come to your workshop.

Workshops for volunteers

The training of volunteers has become an important part of many community activities. Workshops are now offered for people willing to do tasks for nothing: training guide dogs, driving the partially sighted, working with immigrant families, and many other roles.

As a generalisation, workshops for groups like this are a pleasant occasion, although the same issues of not wanting to talk can arise as with any group. See p. 153 for more on the silent attender.

Workshops for young people

As our examples in this book show, although we are assuming that most workshops are directed at adults, this is not necessarily the case. If you are called on to prepare a workshop for children, here are some considerations.

Attention span

Anyone who has worked with people under the age of twenty will reinforce the message that the younger the attenders, the shorter their attention span. On the other hand, the fact that adults are able to sit and listen for longer periods shouldn't mean that presenters take advantage of their patience. Variety of activity helps learning for all ages.

Experience

Speaking generally again, the older the participants, the more life experience they have accumulated. However, they are not the only ones who bring contributions. When workshops are held for young people who have suffered physically or emotionally, they will bring with them plenty of experience on which to build input and activities. We have heard of workshops for children in these and other sad categories, where the specific experience of the attenders may be greater than that of the presenter:

Siblings of cancer patients
Sufferers of specific medical conditions
Survivors of various forms of abuse
Unaccompanied refugee minors
Bereaved adolescents.

Social aspects

Children enjoy activities which have a strong social element. When they are being chosen to attend a workshop, suggest that organisers invite at least two children from each school or area, so that participants arrive knowing at least one other person there. One child who attended a two-day event was asked if she had felt at all homesick at night. She replied:

'No. Because my friend was with me.'

Takeaways

For young people, anything they can take home from the workshop will help to reinforce their learning in the following days and weeks. This is particularly true if the resource has activities that can be completed later.

Workshops for special needs learners

Although details of workshops for special needs learners are outside the scope of this book, the principle of building on participants' experience and strengths remains. We recently heard of a computer workshop designed for young people with special learning needs. One of the attenders, who had Downs Syndrome, was invited to be a presenter at some following workshops because of his empathy with other learners, and also, of course, because of what he had learned. If you are not experienced in working with such groups, seek advice from a professional, or perhaps a previous trainer of the participants.

▶ Locations for workshops

Of course, workshops can be held in as many different locations as there is space to fit people in. If they are intended to be closely linked to people's places of work, then why not hold them right there? That saves money and time. One counter-argument is that going away to a 'retreat' type of loca-tion is often seen by employees as a treat. But the environment can also have a major impact on the learning that takes place. For example, for business people, meeting in an art gallery might offer a refreshing change that could encourage some 'out of the box' thinking. Here are comments from people who attended off-site and on-site workshops.

'Part of the atmosphere of the workshop was made by the fact that we were taken to another location. It might sound superficial, but just sitting in a room with a view of the water seemed to make us all more relaxed than we would have been back at the office.'

'I've attended workshops at my actual workplace and off-site. My definite preference is for the latter. When we were in room next door to the office, people kept popping back there between sessions to catch up with things. It spoiled the flow of the day.'

'The only benefit of not going "outside" was that our colleagues who were not at the workshop could see that we were not away having a "fun" time. That doesn't seem like a strong enough reason '

In summary, it seems that the advantages for having workshops away from the daily workplace are both organisational and affective.

Informal contexts

Workshops can also be held in more informal contexts. One example of this is the 'brown bag' workshop, held during people's lunch breaks. The mood of the workshop will be affected by at least two factors, one of which is that time is likely to be short. Once the brown bags have been emptied people may be heading back to the worksite. Another factor is that with people's hands (and mouths) kept busy with their lunches, it's not as easy to organise activities. One suggestion would be to offer a short talk during 'brown bag' time with the promise of a later workshop if people are interested in the topic. Another way around this is to make more use of silent tasks, such as 'think about two ways to respond to this customer ...', or 'of the three options on the board, which would you choose?'

Fieldtrips

For some practical subjects a field trip may the obvious choice. It allows people to see:

Workers doing regular projects in their own contexts
Machinery or other equipment which is too cumbersome to move
Different stages in a work cycle.

However, field trips can also be useful for other subjects, as the following vignette shows.

Fieldtrips are certainly not an easy option. In the example above, it would have taken considerable time and effort to arrange transport and to find the local speakers.

Online

Delivering workshops online has a number of obvious advantages, such as the ability to accommodate people from distant locations who might otherwise be unable to attend. It also comes with a number of challenges for the facilitator. We deal with these in detail in the section on 'Delivering workshops online' (pp. 123–31).

At conferences

Workshops held during a conference need to be even more time conscious than in other venues. Although the responsibility of organising the room before and afterwards will not be yours, keeping to time most certainly will be. There is nothing more annoying for the next workshop organiser than to find that the room is not clear until ten minutes late. That is why some procedures are common at conferences.

1 A person is appointed to chair each workshop and to alert organisers to the need to stop.
2 People who want to talk with the presenter are invited to do so outside the room afterwards.

▶ Workshops in other countries

There may be occasions when you are called on to travel to another country to conduct a workshop. In this section we consider the context where you are in your own country, but you have been told beforehand that the attenders come from many different countries. A couple of questions arise in a mixed group like this.

What variations are there in the way people like to learn new ideas?

How far is it possible to match their learning styles with your teaching style? Here are some considerations.

A range of examples

One big benefit of having a range of cultures present is that when you call for examples you will have a rich list as feedback. Acknowledge these as adding to the knowledge of everyone.

You, in turn, can choose *realia* that represent more than one culture.

Speaking through interpreters

The first question to consider is whether or not people's language will be up to understanding what you are saying. When there are only two main language groups then it is common for an interpreter to be present. During your introduction, input and instructions, this person will translate what you say, sentence by sentence. Here are some tips for speaking through an interpreter.

1 Speak only a sentence at a time before leaving time for the interpreter.
2 Avoid anything that would be difficult to translate, such as jokes, local references and very abstruse words.
3 Speak at a measured pace.
4 Let the interpreter know beforehand that he or she is allowed to ask you to repeat.

The interpreter's other role will be during activity time when someone asks a question, to make sure the message is clear both from the questioner to you and vice versa.

If, on the other hand, there are several groups present and they are more comfortable speaking their own languages, during group work consider suggesting that they speak in their own language. When it comes to reporting back they can choose the person most fluent in the main workshop language to do the talking.

Setting goals

Curriculum and course designers usually start with one of three areas of learning:

The content that needs to be covered (or: a focus on input)
The activities that will be used (the process)
The intended outcomes (the product).

A focus on the product, or the outcomes, is helpful to ensure participants know beforehand whether the workshop is likely to meet their needs. It also helps the organiser to evaluate the success of the workshop. In this section we look mainly at the product and consider how to determine outcomes and who sets them. Evaluation of goals is dealt with in the section on 'Evaluating workshops' (pp. 216–19).

Defining goals

Goals can be loosely defined as broad aims or purposes. In terms of a workshop, a goal might answer the question for a workshop organiser or attender, such as 'What is my purpose in organising or attending this workshop?'

This leads to the question of who sets the goals and writes them out for others to understand. When a workshop is being planned, there are usually at least two parties involved in goal-setting: the person initiating the event and the person at the front once it starts. That is an over-simplification because it could be that the initiation comes from a group of people. This is most likely to happen when the workshop is tailored for a particular workplace. Many people will be involved in suggesting topics and goals, even if they do not express their ideas in terms of the word 'goal'.

Another possible answer to who defines the goals is that if there are to be several presenters, they may all want to have a hand in setting the goals, or at least have a chance to see them before planning their sessions. In addition, there are the goals written some time beforehand by potential workshop attenders. At the end of one workshop the organiser followed her speech of thanks to the presenter with words like these:

'You need to let me know what topics you want for future workshops. I might dream up ideas that don't interest you. Email me your ideas any time.'

A more focused approach could be to email a survey asking for suggestions, possibly including some potential topics, but leaving space for their suggestions.

Finally, there is goal-setting by observation. An employer observes staff and notes gaps in their knowledge or skills. This can happen when employers have been with a firm for a long time and haven't been given the opportunity to refresh themselves on new developments.

Describing goals for participants

Once the topic has been decided, then the goals can be worded. Unless these are made clear ahead of time, those who attend and those who organise the event may have different ideas of what that goal might be. The publicity should state quite clearly the intended goal.

Here are some examples from a range of workshops. The first one is deliberately worded to attend to feelings rather than facts.

These workshop sessions are designed for recently widowed seniors. They do not promise to take away the pain, but by working through a process with others who have been through similar experiences, you may come away with a feeling of support and see your grief as something many people experience.

And here is another one on a rather different topic.

In this workshop you will learn about the three key natural aspects that contribute to making a wine distinctive: its grape varieties, its climate, and its terroir. You will learn to identify the influence of each of these on the wine.

Negotiating goals with participants

It is not always possible to invite suggestions from prospective attenders beforehand, and the presenter may feel that the selected topic or level does not meet the needs of the participants. Experienced presenters usually prepare additional materials so that they can give participants a choice over content, level or activities (we deal more with this in the section on participant issues, p. 145).

Although it can be challenging, especially for organisers new to workshops, it is a good idea to go over the intended outcomes of the workshop at the start and to give participants a chance to comment. It is much more useful to find out at the start that the audience members have just completed another workshop on one of the topics you were planning to cover, rather than afterwards! You may have the outcomes stated in educational jargon, but in going through them you should use more everyday language including, perhaps, an example or two. Here is the experience of a colleague who teaches computer programming:

> 'I have learned over the years that the best workshops I give are those where the participants are really interested in the subject. One way of making sure they are, that I use, is to briefly show them three products I created, at the start of the workshop, and ask them which one they are most interested in learning more about. I then use that as the main source.'

▶ Types of goal

So far, we have spoken about the terms 'goals' and 'outcomes' only, but you probably know a range of other terms used to describe different types of learning and teaching intentions.

Although they are not always used in this way, traditionally the words 'goals' or 'aims' describe something broad, such as those in the paragraph on 'Describing goals for participants' above (p. 77).

Objectives are more like an operationalisation of these goals or aims. They describe what the aim seeks to achieve in terms of smaller units of learning, and describe learning in terms of observable behaviour. Table 2.4 shows one general example. You could add others from your own specialisation.

Table 2.4 Goals

Goal (or aim)	Sample outcome	Measured by ...
To introduce new techniques for ...	To practise a specific technique within a time limit	Task completion

To further illustrate the difference between goals and objectives:

Goals are broad; objectives are narrow.
Goals are general intentions; objectives are precise.
Goals are intangible; objectives are tangible.
Goals are abstract; objectives are concrete.
Goals can't be validated as is; objectives can be validated.

There are different types of objectives. You will sometimes see a distinction between:

Coverage objectives ('this workshop will cover interrogations of three types of suspects')
Activity objectives ('participants will offer a short presentation')
Involvement objectives ('participants will engage in discussions')
Mastery objectives ('participants will be able to ...')

Objectives can be overt ('participants will be able to define ...') or covert ('... understand') and they can be short-term or long-term.
Another traditional way of categorising objectives is according to:

Knowledge
Skills
Attitudes

It is also important to run them through a filter by asking questions such as these:

Can it be measured? Under what circumstances?
Is this reasonable for the time available?

As with learning outcomes, we can also speak of goals that lead to knowledge or skills, or, as we have seen before, goals relating to feelings. Social goals relate to other people that one might meet at a workshop:

'The goal of this workshop is to bring together people who normally work alone in hospitals so that they can exchange experiences and develop future networks.'

Learning outcomes are like goals but focus on the learners and are formulated like a set of statements setting out what the participants should be able to do or understand by the end of the workshop:

'By the end of this workshop you will be able to conduct job interviews following ACD standards.'

'... you will be able to proctor exams independently'

As is clear from the above, learning outcomes have to be demonstrable.

Writing goals, objectives and learning outcomes

You can write goals as follows:

(1) Start with a stem

By the end of the workshop, the participant will have ...
After this unit, the participant will have ...
By completing the activities, the participant will have ...
At the conclusion of the course/unit/study the participant will have ...

(2) Verb

Understood
Created
Compared

(3) Actual product of the activity

The difference between argumentative and expository essays
A customer satisfaction form
Two types of responses to customer complaints

There can be a condition ('given X amount of time', 'given Y tool').
There can be a criterion – speed, accuracy.

Now you try:

A. Judge other people's objectives.
Here are some objectives that have been set for workshops. For each one, suggest whether this meets the criteria set out above. Imagine that they all

start with the words 'By the end of the workshop, participants should be able to ...'

Understand all the principles of ...
Very good / moderately good / not good

Explain one technique to a colleague who has not attended the workshop
Very good / moderately good / not good

Feel more confident about interacting with ...
Very good / moderately good / not good

Develop into a more professional worker
Very good / moderately good / not good

Recite 10 rules for ...
Very good / moderately good / not good

Answer questions from a colleague about the topic of ...
Very good / moderately good / not good

B. Write some goals of your own.
Using Table 2.5:

Think of a long-term goal for a learner you might be working with.
Then break that goal into some small steps. (Column 1)
Plan some activities. (Column 2)
What between-lesson activities could measure the achievement? (Column 3)

Table 2.5 Goals and objectives

1 Short-term goal	2 Lesson activity	3 Measure

Categorising and selecting activities

The activities are at the heart of any workshop and can sometimes give more idea of the content than the actual title, as in one example of a workshop aimed at schoolgirls from 11 to 17 years of age. The title is 'Self Awareness' and the list of activities is a mixture of the factual and the affective, with 'fun' mentioned more than once. The attention of would-be attenders might be caught by the dramatic title and the four pictures, but what could lead them to go or, more likely, to persuade their parents to pay for them to go, is probably the activities, which are broadly described as 'hands-on'.

In this section we start with suggestions for categorising and selecting your workshop activities. We then list a range of common workshop activities for you to adapt to your subject. There are many ways of categorising workshop tasks, but here we explain two:

Bloom's taxonomy
Stages of learning

▶ Bloom's taxonomy

One theoretical base for designing questions as starting points comes from a list designed by Benjamin Bloom, many decades ago, which has stood the test of time.

Questions or tasks based on Bloom's Taxonomy, as it is known, assist users to grasp new ideas at a greater depth than simply remembering and describing them (Petty, 2004). Based on Petty's summary, here are some suggestions for workshop activities which move from the 'relatively undemanding ... [to the] more difficult ... and much more useful' (2004: 8). For the purposes of seeing the progression, let's keep the same scenario throughout the six levels.

Knowledge

At this most basic level, people define or describe what they have just heard. Thus, at a workshop for travel agents where a short DVD has just been shown on 'principles of advertising', there might be the following instruction.

'Turn to the person beside you and say what you think was the speaker's main message.'

Or, on a prepared handout, they could be asked to

'Jot down two ideas you recall from the message.'

before comparing their lists.

Comprehension

The next level of thinking involves tasks such as explaining, classifying, interpreting and describing. In terms of workshop tasks this could mean any of the following.

'Explain a new idea as to colleagues who haven't attended the workshop.'

In a large workshop, if two groups have seen two different presentations, then this task becomes more realistic. A variation on this task is that one of three possible readings is given out to each person. After reading time, they are asked to:

'Find someone who read the same piece as you did. Together plan a three-minute presentation to four other people, describing the ideas you read about.'

There is no reason why the presentation should be only in words.

'Sketch the outline of a poster which includes some graphics and some slogans based on the DVD/reading.'

Classifying new ideas could involve this task:

'List the ideas in two groups: those that are new to you and those that you are practising already.'

Application

The application stage takes new ideas a step closer to what participants will be doing later when they return to their places of work, in other words, from theory to practice. Here are some suggestions.

'Group brainstorm ways of applying some of the new ideas to your context.'

'Choose one of the suggestions made by the speaker/writer and brainstorm situations where that would be easy/difficult in your context. Say why, then listen to suggestions from other group members of how you might overcome these barriers.'

Analysis

Analysing new ideas involves such thought processes as

Compare and contrast
Give reasons
Distinguish between cause and effect

For example, participants can be asked to:

'Draw up a list of similarities and differences between the familiar and the new ideas.'

'Sketch a graphic that shows the relationship between some of the ideas talked about, such as a flow chart moving from *cause* to *event* to *outcome*.'

Case studies also involve analysis. See 'Overview of case studies' (pp. 94–101), for more on writing case studies.

Synthesis

At the synthesis level, people are doing any of the following tasks:

Solving non-routine problems
Working out arguments, counterarguments, rebuttals
Creating hypotheses
Suggesting new ideas.

Any of the following activities would help synthesise content and draw on the strengths of others in a group.

'Form groups of five people, each with one piece of paper. At the top of your page, give one reason why a particular suggestion made so far in the workshop might not work. Then pass the papers around. On someone else's paper put up a counter-argument. Keep going with rebuttals and so on until the page returns to its original writer. Finally, reflect on whether you have now heard some convincing arguments against your concern, or whether your concern has been strengthened.'

'Write some imaginary sentence starters such as 'What would happen if we ...?' to take back to your place of work, as a way of reporting back on the workshop.'

'Read some of these problem situations from authentic sources (such as the media). The solutions have been cut off. If you had been asked your advice, what would you have recommended?
[...]
Now read what was done in real life, and decide which solution you prefer.'

Evaluation

The ultimate test of new ideas collected at workshops is not how original or detailed or sincere they are, but whether they will work in the specific context to which participants are returning. Evaluating is therefore important, because it involves taking everything into account and then judging. Here are some suggested tasks.

'Imagine how this idea [...] might appear to different people at your workplace. In pairs, prepare role-plays in which, on your return, you try to persuade someone from your workplace who is resistant to change. Present the role-play to others as a basis for planning ways of explaining the suggested changes to others.'

If the workshop is on practical skills, the evaluation could come naturally as individuals display their work samples on tables placed around the wall, and others walk around taking notes on strengths and weaknesses. Then feedback can be given to people, one by one, by their peers.

Conclusion

Over the years since the taxonomy was first presented, people have worked at modifying and re-ordering the categories. For workshop purposes neither the order nor the wording of the categories needs to be fixed. For instance, some would say that evaluating should come earlier on, because there's no point in applying something if you consider it irrelevant to your context. Others say that the entire list could be combined in one task. For some groups, that could well work. One general principle is that different ways of thinking help process ideas, and another is that a concept needs to be understood before it is used.

With the tasks suggested, there are still plenty of decisions to be made.

▶ The stages of learning

A second common method of classification is by the stages of learning. Although there can be some overlaps with Bloom's taxonomy, they do not exactly parallel each other, as we will show.

For the purposes of having a thread running through these examples, we have chosen to take all our examples from the same professional field. Let's imagine that you are a health professional running seminars in a rural area of a third world country. Although you are a medical expert, you are not familiar with all the conditions under which the workshop attenders work. Here are some examples of the tasks you could plan. They are presented in three stages:

Processing new ideas
Practising new ideas
Applying new ideas

Tasks for processing new ideas

The first stage of the learning process is meeting new ideas. Traditionally this was done by 'telling', but there are more interesting ways.

The following complaint, which we refer to more than once in this book, applies especially when someone seen as an expert flies in from far away. Workshop attenders who have previously attended only talks and lectures may not appreciate that everything is about discovery learning, whereas they came expecting to be told information by experts. They would rather not waste time trying to discover things for themselves when they could be told much faster. Workshop leaders, on the other hand, say that simply transmitting information is boring or better suited to up-front presentations.

Some of the tasks that follow can be a way of presenting ideas which include new information, but in ways that help people process them.

Find examples for given principles

Here is one suggestion for combining fresh input of principles with local knowledge.

In small groups, everyone is given a list of facts or principles. These could include universal truths, or figures such as:

1 Worldwide, unwashed hands are responsible for ... % of childhood illnesses.
2 The ... vaccine can be administered to babies as young as ... and yet many barriers still stop mothers from taking babies to be vaccinated.

Then each group brainstorms examples, such as.

1 What are some reasons why parents don't encourage children to clean their hands?
2 List as many barriers as you can. Then share examples of how you could help overcome these barriers.

Finally, the groups combine their examples. These can be listed on a board or typed up later and distributed to the group, who will then have locally relevant examples grouped under the new headings.

Categorise examples

This task type can work well if you take a collection of pictures or photographs to the workshop to illustrate your point. For a medical workshop, these could be a collection of photographs of problems such as skin rashes, cuts or other injuries, and so on. Participants can group the pictures in various ways, such as:

Preventable/non-preventable injuries, illnesses ...
Short-term/long-term effects
Recovery requires medication/operation/time
Within/beyond budget

This classification task can be followed by discussion as people move around the room looking at other people's ideas. Finally there can be suggestions from the leader.

Match cause and effect

Coloured cards have words or phrases written on them.

Dehydration / nausea / brittle bones / running eyes

These have to be matched with cards of a different colour, each listing one possible cause. Of course, the easier ones are matched first and then others are worked out by a process of elimination.

Compare and contrast

This can work with two or more pictures, maps, graphs … For example:

'Look at these two maps of rural areas in two different countries. You can see symbols for wells, schools, clinics. You can also see the mortality rates for each. What differences and similarities do you see?'

Predict

Participants are given some incomplete data, such as graphs, and are asked to predict what the missing information might say. This works well for material such as …

GRAPHS

'The following graph shows mortality by decades in [X country], correlated with family size. Predict the missing information.'

WHO SAID WHAT?

'Here are the responses to a questionnaire asking who would consider giving up smoking if they were given free trial patches.

I tried once but it was too stressful.
My father is dying of lung cancer and he says I should try to give up.
I'd like to give up before my children are old enough to notice.'

Tasks for practising new skills

Here participants are taking the new ideas and trying them out in a controlled environment.

Interviews

There are two purposes for asking participants to conduct interviews with one another. One is the process and the other is the content. This can work well as a paired activity when workshop attenders actually need to practise the skill of interviewing, for any one of these reasons:

A job interview

Investigating a child's unexplained injuries that have led to hospital admission

An employment problem

A survey of local opinions on some suggested change in accident and emergency arrangements.

For each of these situations the participants could be provided with a template that gives broad suggestions for each question but leaves out details.

One extra dimension to this activity is to have an observer taking notes during the interview. At the end of the interview, the three people debrief.

What went well?

Any problems?

Suggestions for next time?

Finally, they list advice to others on how to do this type of interview, and present this at a report-back session to the whole workshop.

Role-play

Provide scenarios which are as close as possible to difficult situations that people may face in their place of work. Here are a couple of examples:

(1) Workplace decision making

'You are part of a small advisory group who have been asked to provide suggestions for allocating funds from next year's budget. There are three divisions at your workplace, each needing increased funding. Appoint a chairperson and assign people to different divisions.'

(2) Managing a queue

'You are taking your turn working at the counter of your health clinic. Your job is to assign people with numbers and then call them up when their turn comes. However, people are constantly coming back to the desk to ask for priority treatment.'

Projects

For longer workshops, say those lasting more than a day, there is the chance to do some longer projects. For example:

Design an advertisement in your own language persuading school children to accept and use toothbrushes and toothpaste.
Create an action timeline for new ideas you have met in this workshop.

Preparing a presentation

Some workshop participants, who come as representatives of their workplaces, may be called on to present ideas from the workshop to colleagues once they return. A workshop can conclude by providing materials for making parts of a presentation. This could include:

A Powerpoint presentation
A handout
Summaries of group discussions
Lists of priorities as decided by participants
Contact details of all participants, so that they can continue collaborating.

If done as a group task, this can mean that everyone has a ready-to-go presentation when they leave.

YOUR TURN

The ideas listed so far have all been from one area of expertise, but we have seen them work for other workshops on widely ranging topics such as:

Budgeting
Foster care
Rural development
Parenting
Aged care
Community planning

To see whether the ideas would work for you, try listing your own examples under some of the headings.

Tasks for applying new ideas

Once new ideas have been met and understood, they need to be applied to the workshop attenders' own contexts. The difference between this stage and practising is that now there is less control by the presenter, as people take ideas and put them into their own, various contexts.

Lists

Lists can be prompted by sentence starters such as these:

'If an aid programme wanted suggestions for gifts to our district, our suggestions would include ...'

'Some of the reasons why parents do not insist on children taking medicine are ...'

'For me, the hardest part of running a weekly clinic in the villages is ...'

As with the other topics, these would need following up, but instead of addressing concerns thought up elsewhere, the presenter could draw on experience to make suggestions.

Prioritising

New ideas will go nowhere if they can't be applied later back at people's places of work, for whatever reasons. As one example, it often happens that participants feel overwhelmed by all the new ideas. Following one of the feedback sessions, and while responses are still on the board or Powerpoint, it can help if everyone determines some sort of priority list for action. These lists can be organised in various ways:

'When you look at the list of points on the board you may be thinking that some are too complicated or too expensive. Grade the suggestions in one of these ways:

From least to most urgent
From least to most feasible
From most to least difficult to implement
From cheapest to most expensive
From fastest to most time-consuming.'

If participants are working with people from a similar context they can then take the list to the next step, where they suggest a time line for implementation.

Problem solving through case studies

People work in pairs or groups to solve a problem. This goes well if the case studies presented are genuine. Without breaking confidentiality it's possible to turn the examples from last month's workshop in one place to something useful for the next place. For example:

'A community nurse reported that although it was policy to follow up the wellbeing of new-born babies and their mothers in their own homes, she often found that nobody was at home at the time arranged.

How many reasons could there be for these absences?
What possible suggestions could work, for making sure that there is ongoing contact between nurses and new-borns with their mothers?'

Workshop activities

► **Ice breakers and energisers**

An ice breaker is any short activity held at the start of the workshop. Its purpose is to lower any affective barriers that may exist within a particular group. The rationale is that when people share something about themselves, and when they hear about others, they are more likely to have a positive attitude towards the group, the workshop and the presenter, and to want to work together. Although this is what the research tells us, many participants (and presenters) have divided opinions on ice breaker activities, perhaps as a result of some presenters taking such activities a bit too seriously and dedicating considerable amounts of time to them. Here are some general considerations:

► Firstly, the time spent on an ice breaker activity should be in proportion to the length of the workshop. A two-hour workshop may not need an ice breaker activity at all. A week-long retreat style workshop may dedicate two hours to one.
► Although the purpose is to 'break through' participants' reluctance to open themselves up to the group, this should not be done at all costs. Some participants simply take some time to feel comfortable in a group.
► Choice of activities should consider the age and background of the participants. Silly games may work with teenagers but may not be suitable for older participants.
► Be careful with activities that require participants to touch one another. This may not be acceptable in all cultures or even age groups.
► Although many ice breakers involve participants sharing something personal, be careful about the level and type of information you ask them to share. A safer option is to ask participants to share something about their opinion on a professional topic, rather than a highly personal one, or about a fictitious situation or other person (such as 'What should colleague X do in this situation?').

A Google search will bring up many examples of specific activities.

Energisers are short activities designed to reinvigorate participants. They are an important, and often under-used, element, especially of longer workshops. There is a great deal of research that has shown the negative impact that prolonged periods of sitting still can have on learners' concentration and ability to remember new information. Workshops have the advantage over some other forms of teaching in that they involve more moving around, but it is still important to consider whether participants are getting enough opportunity to 'stretch their legs'. One of us often teaches in an institution where there is a small park near to the workshop classroom. Some of the activities, such as doing short interviews, lend themselves to being done while walking around, which always seems to help the participants to keep up their attention.

Some presenters seem to have developed energisers into an art form with frequent exercises. 'Brain gym' is a series of exercises specifically designed to energise not only the body, but also the mind. Mostly these involve coordination exercises such as raising your left knee to your right elbow. They have been shown to increase concentration and participation.

Obviously such activities need to be done with consideration for the expectations and abilities of the audience.

▶ Overview of case studies

Case studies, or case analyses, 'have had a long history and have played major roles in a number of different disciplines', as Dean Brown and Rodgers point out (2002: 21). Case studies are said to have been used at Harvard Law School since 1870 (Richards and Farrell, 2005: 126). In law schools and conferences, real-life examples allow discussions of how to respond to specific incidents. In medical settings, doctors in training or doctors attending professional development workshops can talk about their options when facing common or rare conditions. Business conferences use cases from their own and other countries as the basis for planning.

The underlying principle is problem solving through sharing ideas, based on the word 'heuristic', which describes a method that allows people to learn something for themselves. Case studies are one way of helping in the process of learning for oneself. In this section we look at definitions and examples of case studies and ways in which they can be used in workshops. We also mention issues such as confidentiality when authentic examples are being used.

What makes a 'case'?

The first step in writing a case study is to have an actual situation where something needs to be done. Veteran workshop presenters try to keep a bank of these examples, but they are also alert for topical illustrations. The 'case' could be a problem that needs solving, or it could be a process that needs to move to the next step or a viewpoint which calls for a response. Ideally the solution or the step should not be too obvious and could in fact have more than one option. It is up to the workshop participants to suggest what this might be.

The source of the example is normally found by the presenter beforehand, but it is also possible for participants to submit their own examples, particularly if the workshop has a break or extends for more than a day, so that the presenter has time to set the 'study' part.

What are some other sources of data? Anything published recently in the professional area of the workshop should be relevant and authentic. However, if the example is a negative one, beware of making it seem like an attack on one special interest group which could be represented within the workshop.

A second source is personal experience. This can sometimes be put into the third person, so that people don't feel embarrassed about offering criticism. Perhaps change names and locations.

Then there are ideas from previous workshops. Often an example raised in one workshop can be an interesting starting point for the next one, with, once again, the proviso about anonymity. One exception to the 'Be authentic' suggestion is that occasionally an example is deliberately exaggerated for effect, including humour. (But see below, for a warning about humour!)

Not everything has to be already available. Presenters sometimes choose to invent their own 'case' so as to avoid the suggestion that someone known to participants is the anonymous person in the example. In this case the characters in the 'story' can represent different levels of the workforce and include a range of people. Fortunately the decade has passed where participants would go through, counting the relative number of male and female pronouns in cases, but the general principle of making sure that many groups are represented still stands.

A 'case' is typically short and easily understood. It can include some direct speech, as in the following open-ended illustration.

'A sales rep came back to his base and reported a problem to his supervisor. "Yesterday I was ... What should I do next time that happens?"'

So far we seem to be suggesting that a case must be a short, written paragraph. On the contrary, a video clip can be an interesting lead-in to a discussion of questions. Try stopping the clip before a solution has been reached. If the workshop involves a practical skill, then work samples could be used as the case. For example:

'The following samples were submitted to you for comment. Some are clearly in line with the machining principles your workplace requires; others are not. You have been asked to give individual feedback but one-to-one rather than in front of everyone else. Work in pairs to do this activity.'

Of course, many case studies are more comprehensive than those outlined above. For example, participants could be given all the information relating to a problem faced by a company and be asked to solve the issue. One way of making such case studies interesting, and a good way of differentiating your instruction to cater to participants with different interests or levels of experience in class, is to visualise an activity based on case studies as shown in Figure 2.1.

In the figure you can see that different aspects of the case study can be given to participants, or even different aspects to different participants. For example, the solution to the problem could be provided to one group, but not the context. Similarly, the relevant problem could be given but not the required background information, which participants would then have to locate.

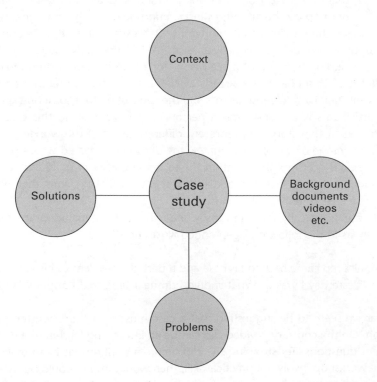

Figure 2.1 Aspects of a case study

What can go wrong?

They know it already

Some 'cases' do the rounds with only the names and locations changed. There's nothing worse than choosing an example that seems fresh but anonymous, only to have someone at the workshop say, 'I've heard that story before. It's an urban myth.' These 'myths' used to do the rounds long before the Internet, so we can't blame that medium.

One of us had an interesting experience when presenting an example to an international group in our own country. I had taken the trouble to choose an example from a recent book by a widely known international publisher. It referred to an innovation in the home country of some of the workshop attenders and I made sure it was a positive example. As we started looking at it there was a mini-flurry in one corner. Two people were using their electronic dictionaries to look up the right word so that they could explain something to the rest of us. It turned out that the innovator being written up as an outstanding example for something, had just shot to national fame for something else and had recently been imprisoned. So much for current relevance.

Culturally specific humour

In an attempt to make a case interesting, the presenter sometimes introduces humour. Unfortunately humour doesn't always travel well, either across cultures or between different groups within a workshop.

Once I attempted to liven things up by illustrating a point with a cartoon. Never again. One participant took umbrage at the point of the joke and said he failed to see why everyone else was laughing. He felt his culture was being ridiculed (although there was nothing at all in the picture to link it to his group). Some people who have heard that story have responded by saying that things would be very bland if people could never laugh at themselves. True, but I have been very aware since then of the distinction between laughing at oneself and appearing to laugh at a particular group.

The example is too genuine

The issue of confidentiality is one to keep in mind, particularly when the illustration is of something rare. Although a breach of trust in medical examples is often talked about, situations at any place of work can be confidential. Ask yourself some questions.

▶ Could these people be easily identified?
▶ Would changing some details make the story more general?

▶ Is the source in the public domain anyway, so that anonymity is not an issue?

▶ Do I need to ask someone's permission first?

The study

The 'study' part of a case study usually consists of a series of discussion questions. The discussion on Bloom's levels of questioning, earlier in this chapter, sets out ideas for wording these at a range of levels. Participants, usually working in small groups, analyse the situation and make suggestions for action. They should be ready to justify their suggestions to people from other groups later.

In summary, the discussion tasks usually start by inviting people to state the problem, acknowledging that it may not say the same thing to everyone.

'What seems to be the problem here?'

'How might it look differently to Person A and Person B?'

The next step is to move towards a solution.

'How many options can you see for solving the dilemma?'

'Which would you recommend, and why?'

To quote just one context, in teacher education a case study or case analysis 'involves collecting information over time about a teaching situation and using that information to better understand the situation and to derive principles from it' (Richards and Farrell, 2005: 126). However, case studies are used far more widely than with teachers. As this section aims to show, case studies can be an important part of workshop learning. They will often be presented to participants by the facilitator, although with some skill they can be collected on the spot as people give their own examples, and used as data for participants to analyse.

In summary, through examples from a range of work and community contexts, case studies are a way of allowing people to examine their own beliefs and practices. Through case studies they consider the relationship between what they know (have learned) and what they do (in their current places of work).

Case studies from one context

The scenarios in Figure 2.2 are summarised from Pitt (2005). They were used at a workshop for tutors who were working one-to-one teaching English to adult learners who were former refugees and immigrants. Participants were asked to read the scenarios of three members of the same extended family and then answer the following questions in small groups:

'What motivation might each person have for asking to have a home tutor?'

'What reading and writing skills does this person have already?'

Grandfather was educated in the Punjab before Independence. He emigrated to East Africa and then to England. He reads the name on the bus to take him where he wants to go. In the street he takes notice of advertising signs. At the community centre he skims through a newspaper in English to get general news. When his grandson comes home from pre-school he reads him a children's book in English.

Grandmother had little formal education. Sometimes to catch the bus she recognises the shape of the word because she has seen it often. She has developed a good memory. She also recognises some of the advertisements on the bus.

Mother takes her son to a pre-school and brings home notes from the school for her husband to read in the evening. He is a factory supervisor who was brought up and educated in Britain from an early age.

Figure 2.2 Workshop scenarios

VIGNETTE

'I have sat in on some other people's conference workshops as a preparation for some I'll be running myself before long. One thing I notice is that some workshops are pretty much like the formal talks at the conference. Doesn't the word "work" suggest that participants are meant to do something?'

Following the discussion in twos and threes, the participants fed back their responses, which the facilitator then linked with the theory. The following steps show one possible sequence.

1 Ask participants to report back their ideas. As they do this, summarise their responses in the format you want to build on later (see the example in Table 2.6).
2 Return to the summary from the discussion, and add theory already prepared. If you use Powerpoint, a good tip is to prepare summaries and quotes for relevant research and theory in advance, and have these appear when discussing participants' answers. If you do not wish to reveal the content before your participants give their feedback, and as you do not know in what order they will mention the different points, you could use various buttons with hyperlinks, which can be clicked to add or

Table 2.6 Summarising participants' responses

Purposes for reading and writing (reported back by groups)	Examples of materials (provided by facilitator)	References, on handout, to aspects of theory
Social exchanges	Printouts of email or chat exchanges	
To achieve an outcome	Invitations Queries about products	
Personal enrichment	Personal experiences by previous participants	
To give and understand information	Manufacturers' instructions	

remove specific content. By using letters (for example, 'M' for 'motivation') to remind you, you do not have to reveal the keywords or content to your participants first. Alternatively you could simply have a number of buttons in different colours and include a legend for them in your Powerpoint notes. (Remember: you can see notes on your computer screen that are not projected onto the main screen. See your Powerpoint help files under 'presenter notes', for more information.)

3 Show sample materials illustrating how to implement the teaching of communication skills for the different purposes mentioned by the participants.

4 Point participants to references already on their handouts.

Table 2.6 is a sample of how you could summarise participants' responses in the above scenario

Conclusion

We mentioned the underlying principle of case studies as encouraging people to learn for themselves. Case studies stop short of providing heuristics (a set of rules for solving problems) but they do provide tools that give people practice in solving problems for themselves.

▶ Discussions

Situations suitable for discussions

Petty (2004: 209) suggests that discussions are particularly helpful in three types of situation, which we now summarise for the workshop context.

1 To share opinions and experiences

When people bring an interesting variety of ideas and experiences to a workshop, discussions are a way of making these known. Therefore they are probably best placed near the beginning and probably with groups from dissimilar backgrounds. The discussion task can invite people to evaluate a statement or a suggestion or, in a practical workshop, a piece of work.

Questions for this purpose could have starters like these:

'In your experience ...'

'What examples have you heard of relating to ...?'

2 For non-factual topics

Such topics could relate to what Petty classifies as 'values, attitudes, feelings and awareness, rather than exclusively factual material' (2004: 209). Topics that come to mind are:

Community views on proposed district changes
Drafting regulations relating to workplace behaviour
Addressing stereotyping in an institution.

There is no point in asking people's views about something which is already compulsory.

Questions to begin discussions of this sort could have such starters as these:

'What do you see as the advantages and disadvantages of ...?'

'What do you see as the most/least effective response to ...?'

It goes without saying that closed questions would not be helpful here.

3 To show participants how to express opinions

Some workshops have as their goal to make participants feel stronger about expressing their views. This could apply to workshops for:

Adults who have left school without qualifications
Marginalised groups in society
Survivors of trauma.

Giving focus to discussions

Some facilitators are concerned that discussions can be unfocused, but a set of clear, guiding questions can usually help you avoid this. The following list gives some examples of questions that were asked at the start of a workshop on measuring learners' progress.

Table 2.7 Bloom's categorisation with our workshop examples

Bloom's category	Example
Knowledge	What forms of assessment are used in your department?
Comprehension	Could someone explain to the others the difference between formative and summative assessment?
Application	Look at this sample from a recent test. How might you use this with a class of first-year high school language students?
Analysis	Look at the list of competencies supplied by the Ministry of Education. Can you suggest a way of categorising them in order to plan a syllabus?
Synthesis	How might you introduce the ideas from today's workshop in the context of your present curriculum?
Evaluation	In your groups, can you use some of the principles we have looked at today to improve on some of the items from this list of test items?

Concerns of workshop presenters

QUESTION

'I sometimes run workshops in countries where the participants are interested only in practical "teaching tips". As soon as I mention theory or research they switch off. Still, I think it is important to explain why something works or doesn't. How can I balance this?'

Concerns such as the one listed above can be attended to through workshop discussions. A situation and its potential solution need not be referred to in theoretical terms, but rather, the theory is integrated into the discussion points. In the example in Figure 2.3, participants in a community language teaching workshop on integrating reading and writing in lessons were given the information and discussion questions shown in the figure. The tutors were working one-to-one with adult learners.

I talked with my student about setting goals so that we could measure his progress that way. However, he insisted that setting goals was my job. 'You are the expert.' Should I just go ahead and set the goals?

How many options can you suggest for this tutor?

_____

_____

_____

Which would you recommend, and why?

_____

_____

_____

Figure 2.3 Example of a discussion question sheet

Organising discussions

So much for the thinking that happens in workshops. What about the instructions and organising of the discussion groups? Petty (2004: 209) has suggestions here as well. In summary, these include.

Seating arrangements

People need to be able to see one another's faces and hear what is said without straining. Traditionally, U-shaped seating works well for audibility.

Brief the participants

Give some brief guidelines at the start as to the intended length of the discussion and its purpose. The purpose can be related to the process ('to get to know one another's strengths or opinions') even when there is no intended group outcome.

Brief the leader

Even if the leader has no more expertise than others, he or she can be supported with some guidelines, such as a reminder to encourage more than one view and a suggestion of how to discourage one or two people from dominating. This latter can be done non-threateningly by making eye contact with someone else who looks as if they want to say something, and then, perhaps, naming that person.

▶ Analysis

Analysis is a form of critical reflection that relies on our ability to question our teaching and ourselves as teachers, our beliefs, and our attitudes. It involves 'articulating ... beliefs and comparing these beliefs to their actual classroom practice and underlying beliefs' (Farrell, 2007: 9). The ability to analyse one's teaching lies at the heart of teacher development, as without self-awareness and knowing how to act on it, future self-improvement will be difficult or impossible. Teachers, like all professionals, need to learn to 'step back' from their own practice. Workshops offer a great opportunity to do this in a safe environment and with the benefit of support from the facilitator and from peers.

Workshop topics often relate to the practical aspects of participants' work, answering 'how' questions. However, professionals are increasingly being encouraged also to reflect on the 'why' questions, such as why some particular ethnic groups succeed in society while others don't. Critical theory, a wide field, 'questions things we have taken for granted. In so doing it seeks to unmask the ways in which power is exercised by one group to the disadvantage of other groups' (Carter and Nunan, 2001: 220). Wigglesworth (2003) groups factors affecting group, or collective, learning into four categories: cultural, social, educational and individual. Each of these could be introduced in workshops via a variety of media, as the sample materials and activities listed in Table 2.8 suggest.

Table 2.8 Critical analysis activities

Factors	Source of material	Workshop activity
Cultural	A study of learning styles across different cultural groups	Detect bias in the research questions.
Social	Case studies of educational underachievement in low-income families	Identify factors leading to underachievement. Research options for change.
Educational	A school ranking by student achievement on a national test	Determine reasons for the ranking results and suggest an alternative measurement.
Individual	Interviews with successful students	Review, critique, and adapt the study for use in the local school.

Critically questioning one's own professional role is potentially threatening and requires a degree of sensitivity on the part of the facilitator. Below, we offer some suggestions to introduce this aspect of professional development into a workshop.

Critical approaches to learning and teaching

Recent years have seen a lot of interest in so-called 'critical approaches' to learning and teaching. Often these investigate racial, political, or gender biases in educational policy and in individual classrooms. Questioning our own teaching in this light is particularly challenging as it touches on very personal beliefs, some of which people may wish to ignore or at least not have exposed in a public setting. Nonetheless, if done with tact, dealing with these topics can be extremely informative and lead to great insights among participants.

Basing a workshop around principles of critical thinking such as these would be especially important if the participants were decision makers. Inviting them to look at the attitudes of third parties makes the activity less confrontational, as suggested in the following sample, in which participants are invited to see themselves as members of a selection panel for a language teaching position at their institution.

Sample task 1 – Role-play

This role-play task is shown in Figure 2.4.

Sample task 2 – Materials evaluation

Another form of analysis is through evaluating sample materials. McGrath (2002) speaks of 'pre-use', 'in-use' and 'post-use' of materials evaluation. Workshops can be helpful at the second and third of these stages if teachers are given notice to bring samples of materials they plan to use or have already used. The workshop facilitator provides evaluation criteria.

In a study of our own (Reinders and Lewis, 2006) we suggested the framework shown in Table 2.9, for selecting materials for self-study (for example, as offered through a library or a resource/tutorial room). In a subsequent workshop, participants were asked to choose three resources from several available classroom materials and apply the framework. The teachers then had to discuss the results together and come to an agreement on their answers. This led to interesting discussions and showed considerable differences. What for some was a clear description of the student level (second feature in the table), to others was not clear at all. Analysing what makes a

Appointments committee role-play

As one member of a six-person appointments committee you have been asked to consider the interview summaries from three candidates who have made the short list. As preparation for the committee discussion, each of the six members has been asked to read the summaries and make notes. You detect certain attitudes in the summaries presented to you at the start of the meeting, which make you uncomfortable.

1 Read the summary below.
2 Make some discussion notes.
3 Join with the other committee members and discuss your concerns.

CANDIDATE X presented as a smartly dressed woman of indeterminate age. She has had ten years' experience of professional work in her home country and is now a citizen here. Her English was fluent and correct although highly accented. Some members of the panel felt that her dress code was rather formal for everyday work in this country. She ended the interview with an unprompted question about when she could expect to hear the results, which some members of the panel found inappropriate. Her qualifications are suitable for the position.

Figure 2.4 Example of a role-play task

description clear or not to different people turned out to be very useful, as it allowed participants to see that different people interpret materials and instructions in very different ways.

Table 2.9 Evaluating learning materials

Features	Yes/No/Unsure	Comments
Selecting the resource Claims to be suitable for self-study Clearly describes student level Needs to be used sequentially		
Accessing the parts of the resource An index A table of contents A detailed 'map' A glossary Chapter previews or summaries		
The learning process Information summarised Examples provided for tasks Objectives provided for tasks Keys/answers/criteria for tasks		
Learning to learn Notes on the learning process Shows how to set goals		
Other features		

Some interesting results

The framework shown above was used by us in a study investigating to what extent published materials available in a self-access centre were actually useful for self-directed learning. Many of these materials had been written, according to the publishers, specifically for use in, or were 'suitable for' use in, a self-access centre. Surprisingly, our study showed that many of them missed some of the key features one would expect to find, such as clear objectives and answer keys. This showed to us the importance of both critically investigating the claims made by publishers, as well as critically looking at the resources available in your institution to determine whether or not they are suitable for their intended purpose.

▶ Role-play

Role-play is a way of letting people take new ideas and apply them to particular situations relevant to their work or general lives. Role-play is different from drama, where the script is already supplied by the presenter. In role-play, it is up to participants to decide on the wording and actions once a scenario has been suggested to them, although the presenter is available to make suggestions.

An example of role-play instructions in a workshop on customer service would be this:

'You have been approached by a customer who is known to your shop for previous complaints. You suspect that sometimes she takes a product home, uses it and then spoils it so that she can claim a refund. Of course, this is only a suspicion. Prepare two role-plays to show the group two different ways of handling the situation. The group will then recommend which they prefer.'

One of the advantages of role-play is that, as with the example above, it allows for more than one interpretation. As in real life, there is often not just one right answer, although there could of course be more than one wrong one, as the following vignette shows.

VIGNETTE

'I was invited to observe a workshop where people were being trained as social workers. The teacher invited me to join one group as they did a role-play involving someone who had a problem based on some illegal activity. I noticed that the workshop leader didn't actually approach the groups as they were doing the role-play, and once they had all finished there was no time for presentation and feedback. It had seemed to me that some of the things said in the role-play I observed would not have passed the required code of conduct, but this was never commented on.'

Here is an example of a very hands-off approach in an area that seemed to call for guidance. Moving round the room and then later having some presentations followed by feedback would stop this kind of problem.

▶ Show and tell

This type of activity can work well in either of two ways. In the first, people have been asked to bring something to the workshop to show the others. For example, at a weaving or a poetry writing workshop they could bring along samples of their work to show the group, and to have feedback from everyone before the presenter teaches the next skill.

'Show and tell' can also work as a follow-up to some practical work done during the workshop. Making a publicity poster would be one example.

A variation on this type of activity is 'listen and tell'. In a creative writing workshop people often read aloud the work they have done since the last meeting. There may or may not be an 'expert' to comment, but others give advice using some sort of formula such as:

Praise
Recommend
Praise

▶ Interviews

Interviews are a way of drawing on the existing experience of workshop members. They can be used at any of the three stages of learning.

To establish a starting point

In this case the presenter has prepared a short questionnaire beforehand as a means of gauging what knowledge and skills the attenders bring with them. Once people have moved around the room collecting answers, these are reported back numerically and noted in some way so that they can be used again later. The medium can be anything from the old roll of butcher's paper to a computer display on a screen.

Note that this works only for data that is generally statistical, although there is some room for details.

1 Have you had previous experience with …?
2 Was that in the area of …?
   (a)
   (b)
   (c)

To apply new ideas

This type of interview is more open ended, allowing people to talk about ways they would apply the new learning in future. For example:

'What problems can you see in implementing ...?'

'Would you need to discuss possible changes with anyone?'

▶ **Demonstrations, performances and games**

Presenter demonstrations

Demonstrations (or 'performances' for artistic renderings) can be given by the presenter as a practical way to show how a particular tool works in practice, or how a skill is put to use in a 'real' situation. For example, a workshop on customer service skills could involve a demonstration by the presenter on how to conduct a telephone call to a customer. These two examples can work with quite large groups, but in some of the following examples the demonstration needs to have quite a small number of observers. This will affect the number of people you agree to allow into your workshop. (See the section on 'Participant issues', p. 145.)

Demonstrations are particularly helpful where the topic is one that is not easily described, but more easily shown, such as how to create a sculpture from clay. But also for many other skills, demonstrations encourage learning by observations, which is a very powerful way of learning indeed, as shown by the fact that it is how all children learn and develop. Demonstrations also capture participants' attention and have been shown to be one of the most popular types of teaching with learners of all ages. They are therefore useful at times when attention sags.

Another form of demonstration is to show how *not* to do something. This type of demonstration can be both entertaining and educational. In this case it helps to exaggerate a little so that it is quite clear that you are giving a negative, rather than a positive example. Topics that lend themselves to this kind of humorous demonstration often call for another 'actor'. Try to identify an extrovert amongst the group, early in the workshop.

A third variant is to offer two (or more) demonstrations and ask participants to choose which one they preferred, and why. This is not the same as saying one is wrong and the other right. It could be that one is suitable for a specific context and the other for a different context. The demonstration by the presenter can be followed by practice, with small groups giving feedback to one another. (See the section on 'Demonstrations, performances and games', p. 111.)

The impact of demonstrations can be enhanced by

► Making sure you have all the necessary tools, visual aids and so on prepared, to make sure the demonstration is as authentic as possible and that no time is wasted on preparation. Some presenters prepare an object in three stages, to avoid the annoyance of 'waiting for the paint to dry'.

► Making sure participants can see and hear the demonstration well. It may be necessary to do the demonstration more than once, possibly with participants rotating to view the demonstration from different angles.

► Ensuring everyone knows what to look for. Supply questions or give a sheet on which they add details.

► Giving people a chance to predict what will happen. This has been shown to have a positive effect on learning (Crouch, Fagen, Callan and Mazur, 2004).

► Giving an opportunity to reflect and discuss with others on the demonstration.

► Participants receiving insight into the specific steps taken during the demonstration.

Activities could involve participants trying to identify these steps from the demonstration, or participants could be given a series of cards with each of the steps written on them beforehand, then asked to arrange them in the order they think they will be carried out, before having a check afterwards.

Participant demonstrations

Demonstrations can also be done by participants (rather than the teacher) as evidence of having learned the topic at hand. It is one thing for an audience member to put up their hand when asked if they 'feel they now understand how to do ...', but quite another to actually do it. Participants can observe each other with the help of a checklist, for example, listing the different steps that should be taken.

The purpose of the demonstration by participants is not only to gauge how much they have learned but also to let them gain some valuable practice in a safe and supportive environment. An advantage of demonstrations is that everyone needs to make the connection between thought and action, and that people can learn from their mistakes.

Not all educational cultures use demonstrations, in particular by students.

If you feel that some of your participants are not comfortable performing in front of others, perhaps start by working in small groups.

Simulations

Although simulations are similar to demonstrations they are not the same. A simulation is an imitation of a real-life process, one that may not be possible to carry out in its authentic form. A workshop for pilots on emergency landings is unlikely to involve crash landings, but there are ways (e.g. a flight simulator) to imitate such situations. The same applies to surgeons, emergency workers, and so on. Simulations involve the building of a model (such as a computer model of subatomic particles), and this can then be manipulated (for example, by combining different particles to see how they react to each other). It is the manipulation of the object that the word 'simulation' describes.

Computers make creating (virtual) objects and simulating their use easy, and many subjects benefit from the ability to change variables – for example, to visualise the impact of rising temperatures on sea levels, or the transmission of a virus and its subsequent spread. Second Life is an example of an environment that has been used for simulating real-life events in a virtual, 3D environment, and has been implemented in the teaching of concepts from business management to nuclear science.

Successful use of simulations depends on (1) the quality of the model, (2) the range of ways in which it can be manipulated, and (3) the type of feedback participants receive.

Simulations can also involve replicating a social situation, such as a service encounter. A counter can be set up for airline staff to practise checking in passengers. In this case, participants play the role of real life people. In this book we refer to such simulations as 'role-plays' but other books include these under the heading 'simulations'.

Games

Games are different from simulations and role-plays in that they involve some kind of fantasy or make believe. They can, of course, be based on real-life events, people and situations to varying degrees, and require a range of real-life skills. Games are increasingly being recognised for their pedagogical benefits. James Paul Gee, for instance, has identified 36 learning principles that he found to be present in many of the games he investigated. One example of this is the 'Active, Critical Learning Principle'. This stipulates that 'All aspects of the learning environment (including the ways in which the semiotic domain is designed and presented) are set up to encourage active and critical, not passive, learning' (Gee, 2003). In other words, computer games engage learners and get them involved in the tasks at hand. A second principle is the 'Regime of Competence Principle', where 'the learner gets ample opportunity to operate within, but at the outer edge of, his or her resources, so that at those points things are felt as challenging but not "undoable"' (ibid.). If you have ever played a computer game yourself, you will have noticed that if you fail in a task, the game adapts to your level until you do succeed. Similarly, if you succeed too quickly or too easily, new challenges appear. Computers are good at providing this type of adaptive environment.

Games in general also have a number of characteristics that make them potentially useful for various applications in workshops. According to Prensky (2001), games share:

(1) rules
(2) goals and objectives
(3) outcome and feedback
(4) conflict, competition, challenge, and opposition
(5) interaction
(6) the representation of a story.

Many subjects, situations and different kinds of interaction that are considered and practised in workshops have rules and specific goals, and will benefit from clear outcomes and feedback. Different kinds of 'conflict' (e.g., a debate or a competition of some sort) engage participants and encourage deeper learning. As in games, interaction is a major part of workshops where participants are required to collaborate and share, rather than sit passively and listen to the teacher. Although few workshops explicitly use stories, many workshop topics can be related as narratives in which participants play an active role.

Of course, a further major benefit of games is that many participants enjoy them, and they can provide an excellent break from more traditional activities. Many presenters use games as 'energisers' or as ice breakers. (See pp. 93–4, above.)

It is important to choose games that are relevant to the age group and interests of your audience and, as with all workshop activities, to make it clear how the game is relevant to the topic at hand. Some participants, particularly from traditions where games equal children's fun, may resist something that seems like a time waster.

Creation

'Creation' is similar to 'demonstration' but is a term usually reserved for participants' ability to conceive of and execute a product. This could be a flower arrangement in an ikebana workshop, or a letter to a landlord in an English writing class. Successful workshop activities that require participants to create a product set very clear guidelines about what is expected in terms of:

The characteristics of the product (e.g. 'a letter that persuades the landlord to fix the shower')
Any criteria (e.g. '... a letter of at least 500 words')
Any condition (e.g. '... within 20 minutes').

▶ Projects

Short projects are a natural fit for workshops, as they emphasise learning not only by knowing but also by doing. Dewey was one of the first to describe the benefits of active engagement in the learning process as a way to promote learning (1897), and projects have since been shown to be a successful way of implementing this in the classroom, or in our case, the workshop. Some of the benefits include the fact that:

Project-learning is oriented towards attenders
Projects provide practice
Many adults find projects enjoyable
It involves active participation
A project usually involves group work (ideal for breaking down large numbers)
It increases 'ownership' and can help with engaging 'at risk' groups.

Examples of projects that have been completed in workshops include:

Sample publicity posters
A radio broadcast to interest listeners
Making items for free distribution to target groups
Carrying out and collating the results of a survey.

As these examples suggest, when members of a group have different talents, each can contribute something different to the project.

For workshops, projects have the downside that they usually take a long time to complete. In regular courses, projects can run over a period of several weeks or even longer. But project topics can be selected carefully and adapted for a shorter time frame. Alternatively they can be started together but completed after the workshop finishes. Many facilitators, for example, use the morning sessions to lay the groundwork, introduce new concepts, check understanding and so on, and then use the afternoon session for participants to apply what they have learned by completing a small project.

For this to work, several conditions need to be met:

Participants need to have a clear understanding of the intended outcomes (even if these are open-ended).

All necessary resources should be available to complete the project.

Projects need to have some real-life application. In the case of workshops, the best projects are those that not only teach certain skills, but also lead to a tangible outcome that can be applied in their place of work.

Projects require participants to carry out an inquiry or to create something, not simply to carry out tasks from memory.

Good projects have in-built feedback mechanisms. For example, a project to design a new wastewater system will be successfully completed when the system actually works; the feedback is in the result. Alternatively, the feedback can come from end-users, peer-groups, and the facilitator.

All participants need to have a role, and the facilitator needs to watch out for 'loafing' (especially with younger learners), or the tendency of some participants to let others do all of the work, though not always through laziness. Some people have to be encouraged to overcome their shyness.

Sequencing content and activities

Perhaps even more so than with regular presentations or lectures, the order in which you move through your workshop will have a major impact on its success. The main reason is that participants need not only to understand a particular topic but also to be able to apply it. As many skills rely on having acquired other skills, it is important to get the order right, as otherwise participants will not be able to complete some of your tasks.

Some ground rules are to:

▶ move from simple to more complex tasks
▶ move from tasks that require the display of knowledge to those that require analysis (see the section on 'Categorising and selecting activities', p. 82)
▶ mix intensive with more 'relaxed' tasks
▶ mix individual, with pair and group work
▶ include enough breaks, especially between intensive activities.

Unfortunately things are more complicated than this, as often it is difficult to determine how 'simple' or 'complex' a task is, until you have tried it. For this reason it is important to also consider repetition, or the need for most participants to have a chance to encounter new content in more than one context, and to practise new skills multiple times. One way to do this is to draw a 'map' of the workshop for each of the skills or content you want to cover, to remind you of when, how often, and in what contexts it is dealt with. For example, here is a simple diagram of a workshop on language teaching. The topic of 'classroom management' is dealt with three times, in increasing levels of difficulty. The first time, it is dealt with on its own, as a separate topic. The second time, it occurs as part of an activity relating to motivating learners, and finally, participants need to include it in their teaching demonstrations.

Classroom mgmt Intro	Motivation	Teaching demonstration
Scenario task (easy)	Teaching practice (medium)	Integrated skills (hard)

Complexity of content is also about scope, or the extent to which participants need to know the content. For example, in classroom management, as in the example above, there are multiple skills that comprise the ability to handle groups. How many of these will you cover and expect participants to know?

Feedback and assessment

One part of the learning process is to receive feedback on one's effort. Throughout this book we suggest that active participation is important, and one part of any activity, or attempt to do something new, is to be given feedback on one's efforts.

Various metaphors have been suggested for the role of someone giving feedback: football coach, coroner (writing a post mortem at the end), cheerleader, doctor, mountain guide, sheep dog ... A number of purposes have been suggested for giving feedback.

Over to you:

Rank the following purposes for giving feedback in their order of importance for you, with 1 as the most important.

- ☐ to inform participants about their general progress
- ☐ to show that you are a conscientious leader
- ☐ to point out errors
- ☐ for motivational reasons
- ☐ so that people can self-correct better next time
- ☐ to highlight progress since the first attempt

In this next section we consider answers to the questions set out in Figure 2.5.

Options for feedback

Here is a summary of some options for giving feedback on participants' efforts as they practise something new. In considering these options, then, it would probably help if you pictured particular tasks. In Table 2.10 there are some categories you could keep in mind: start by noting under each heading some sample tasks to suit your subject.

- ▶ Presenting something orally to the group
- ▶ Completing a practical task of making something
- ▶ Designing a presentation
- ▶ Preparing graphics

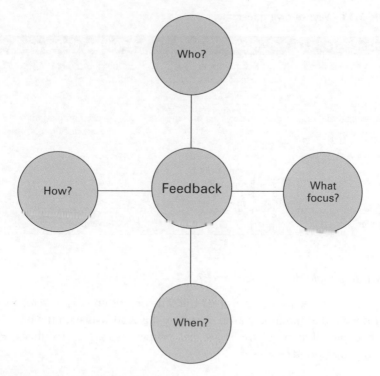

Figure 2.5 Dimensions of feedback

Table 2.10 Options for feedback

Choice 1	Choice 2	Question	Your choice
individually	collectively	Who?	
by the presenter	by peers	Who?	
through marks/grades	through comments	How?	
while people are writing	when the work is finished	How?	
on the form	on the content	On what?	
on what is right	on what is wrong	On what?	

Ways of giving feedback

Some important ways of giving feedback are summarised in Table 2.11.

Table 2.11 Ways of giving feedback

Option	Focus	Prompt to elicit purposes
Peer feedback on ...	Several options for achieving the same outcome	Question: *What is the purpose of ...?*
Self-evaluation (aloud or in writing)	The process of learning to ...	Sentence completion: *I think my first attempt was ...*
Group interviews on ...	Peers interview each person about how they did/made ...	List of questions
Student questions and teacher answers on ...	Features of ...	List advantages and disadvantages

What do people do with feedback?

Whether your feedback is spoken at the time or written later as a follow-up, your hope is that the time you spend doing it is worthwhile. In the box there is a checklist of some of the ways that people respond to feedback. How would you respond?

☐ Look at the grade (or pass/fail) but not the comments.
☐ Read/Listen to the comments but take no action.
☐ Use the comments to do better on the next attempt.
☐ Discuss the feedback with others.
☐ Ask the presenter what the comments mean.
☐ Ask another participant what the comments mean.
☐ Feel happy or unhappy but do nothing about it.
☐ ....

One factor that determines what happens to the feedback is affective. How the feedback is given, and what the person receiving it thinks about the person giving it, both make a difference. Another factor relates to how clearly the feedback is worded. Look at the actual examples in Table 2.12.

Table 2.12 Giving feedback

Comment	Your analysis	Your evaluation of the comment
The ... went quite well but you need to ensure that ...		
Your presentation was too short.		
Please take on board all the comments I made to the earlier people.		
If you work on ... and ... you will be very successful.		
Your ... needed a lot more detail.		
Some sections of your presentation were repetitious and in others the meaning was unclear.		
Except for ... you have the essence of a good ...		

You try:

Analyse each of these comments.

1 Discuss the possible meanings of each of the comments.
2 Evaluate the comments. What do you (not) like about each?

What makes a difference?

For many people, one of the most difficult aspects of giving feedback is balancing encouragement with usefulness. What feedback advice would you give to the presenters who don't know how to give feedback to these people? The teachers of these students?

1 *Someone worked very hard, doing three drafts of each sample, but seemed to make little progress.*

How many reasons can you suggest for this problem?
What feedback would you give?

2 *One person seems not to need this workshop because he is already very competent at all the tasks.*

What feedback do you give?

3 *Another person is also competent but seems bored.*

What sort of feedback might help this student?

Assessing learning in workshops

Assessment is often given little attention in workshops. To the best of our knowledge, no participant has ever 'failed' a workshop! That does not mean that it is not important to establish to what extent learning objectives have been met. There are two basic ways of doing this: (1) asking participants whether they feel they have learned what they wanted; (2) looking for evidence of learning. In most cases, assessment is limited to (1), usually in the form of a feedback/evaluation form handed out at the end of the workshop. We deal with this type of form in the section on 'Evaluating workshops' (p. 216).

Measures of learning (2) can be collected during the workshop or after. During the workshop it is possible to observe participants' ability to:

Carry out a particular task
Create a product
Give a presentation
Explain their choices.

After the workshop, participants could be asked to apply what they have learned and share this with the facilitator and other participants. This could be any of the above and could be recorded in a portfolio, for example (www.eportfolio.org is an example of a free eportfolio, but simple online note-taking programs that can be shared with the workshop facilitator or selected participants can be equally effective; Evernote or Google Documents are two examples).

Some workshops hand out certificates of attendance. In addition, a certificate of accomplishment could be given out if participants can show evidence of achieving the above.

Delivering workshops online

Online classes come with their own challenges and opportunities, and, even more than classes, workshops require some special preparation. It may seem counter-intuitive to offer an activity online that relies so heavily on participant interaction and direct contact between presenter and participant, but online workshops can be a good alternative where face-to-face interaction is not possible. And online delivery is made easier with the right programs that allow for interaction and collaboration. Technology moves fast. As we'll show in this section, it is now possible to have something closely approaching face-to-face interaction.

An extensive discussion of online teaching is outside the scope of this book; for this we refer the reader to the resources listed at the end of this section (p. 131). Here we look at some of the main differences between traditional and online workshops and some of the ways in which they can be conducted.

Why workshops online?

The reasons for choosing online workshops may be positive (such as in response to requests for them) or negative (such as being unable to find a common time and place to meet), organisational (such as money saving) or pedagogic (such as bringing together the best instructors). Whatever the reason, there are situations where an online workshop can be preferable; for example, the presenter may not be able to travel to a particular site or there may be no funding for transportation. One of us recently did an online workshop for teachers in India, which would have been impossible to conduct otherwise. Online facilitation can be a cost-effective alternative in such situations.

Another reason may be that participants are unable to travel, either because of cost, or because work commitments prohibit this. Some organisations are also active on a global scale, with staff and students from around the world, making face-to-face workshops impractical.

Another practical reason relates to last-minute logistical problems. If, for reasons of weather, airline rescheduling or worsening international relations, a presenter is unable to travel, it may be possible at the last minute to set up some substitute arrangement.

There are also some pedagogical benefits to online workshops. For one, it can be less intimidating (for both presenter and participants) to interact online. Research has confirmed that, in particular, less experienced participants may be encouraged to contribute more in an environment where they feel less scrutinised.

Another advantage is that it is easier to have participants complete tasks online as part of the workshop (for example, by visiting a site in a small group), to share content (for example, a Powerpoint presentation they created, or a sales pitch they wrote), and to respond to questions, quizzes and polls. To some extent these online activities can be emulated in a classroom equipped with computers, but online workshops require them for their success.

Online workshops also make it easier to bring in guest speakers for brief contributions, which can be very motivating. Finally, programs that can record the online interaction allow you to post the workshop online for those who were unable to attend, to go over the interactions for ideas for future workshops, and to identify and perhaps share key findings (perhaps the results of a discussion or a brainstorm) with participants afterwards.

YOUR TURN

Have you participated in online workshops or classes? What was the experience like? What did you like about it, and what did you not enjoy? Can you think of ways that the negative elements could have been overcome?

▶ Which program?

The online environment is vital to the success of the workshop, as all participation is done through its interface. Before selecting a web conferencing or collaborative meeting program, ask yourself what types of functionality you require. (A list of common programs is included at the end of this section, p. 131.)

Video

Most of the time you will want to use a webcam so that participants can see you. In some cases – for example, where there is insufficient bandwidth – you may want to keep to audio only, or use the video only for a few minutes at the beginning. Regarding to the issue of bandwidth, if you normally connect to the internet through wifi, it is better, where possible, to connect directly to your router with a LAN cable as this is more likely to provide a stable connection.

Related to this is whether you also want to see the participants. There are two possible scenarios. Where all the participants are together in one room and the presenter is online, it is preferable to install one webcam at the front of the room, pointing at the audience.

Another scenario is where participants are in different locations. Depending on the number of participants, it may not be feasible to see their videos at the same time. Most programs allow you to select individual participants' videos and it may be best to enable this at specific times only, for example to answer one participant's questions.

Good video quality is essential for the presenter and if you think you will deliver workshops online more often in the future, it is worth investing in a standalone webcam. Those built into laptop monitors are usually inferior, resulting in dark and grainy pictures. The quality will depend on the available bandwidth as well, both yours (upload) and the participants' (download), although a lack of upload speed is the most common bottleneck. Check beforehand, and if necessary change the settings for 'frames per minute' until your video appears smooth.

Other considerations include lighting, camera positioning and background. Good lighting is important as most webcams are not great at showing detail in low-light situations. Overhead lighting is usually best. Eye contact is important in online workshops, too, and this can be enhanced by positioning your camera at eye level so that when you look ahead into your screen, participants feel you are looking at them. Finally, choose a background that is not too cluttered, that avoids potentially offensive, or even simply distractingly irrelevant, posters or other personal objects, or movement (such as the view through a window). Many presenters use a bookcase as a background, and that seems to work well.

Finally, on the topic of video, in situations where participants do not have cameras, you may find that it feels unnatural to talk to the computer screen without anyone looking back. In these situations, one of us has developed the habit of imagining the camera lens is a person's eye! A colleague recently shared another suggestion: he had a picture of a group of students just behind his computer monitor, which reminded him he was addressing a real-life audience.

Audio

Clear audio is perhaps the most important requirement for an online workshop. Most microphones built into laptops are not of a good quality and a headset will not only provide vastly clearer sound but will also avoid feedback – the annoying occurrence of interference or echo. It is essential that your participants also use headsets as without this, an 'open mic' (a microphone left on to record) will lead to you (and everyone else) hearing what you say twice, once as you say it, and the second time as it is picked up by the microphone of the participant's computer and then re-broadcast. At the start of the workshop it is usually best to mute all participants' microphones, then explain the procedures for using audio, and then practice this, for example by having participants introduce themselves one by one. This will also allow you to check for any connection problems that individual participants might be experiencing. If participants cannot hear you, use the chat window to communicate with them to resolve the problem.

Not all participants have access to computers or internet and for this reason many programs include the ability to dial in using a telephone (usually a freephone number is included). Obviously this limits the types of interaction possible, but at least it still lets people attend.

Presentation software

Most programs include the ability to show applications from your computer on the participants' screen, such as a Powerpoint or Keynote presentation. This means that you will need to open your presentation slides beforehand, and then select Powerpoint (or whatever other application you choose to use) as the application to share. Participants will then see the slides (but cannot manipulate them).

Be aware that, due to bandwidth problems, sometimes there is a lag when moving from one slide to the next. This can take up to 10 seconds, so do not assume all participants will see what you see on your screen right away. Experienced presenters learn to move to the next slide a few seconds early to avoid this problem.

Screensharing

Screensharing allows you to show whatever is on your computer screen to participants. This is helpful to demonstrate software, for example. Be aware that participants will see everything on your computer, so, as suggested above, you may want to avoid having personal files or pictures on your screen at this time.

File sharing

Some programs allow presenters to easily send files to participants. This can be particularly helpful in the case of virtual breakout rooms (see below).

Interactive whiteboard

A shared whiteboard allows participants to share what they type or draw with others. This is a good tool for brainstorming exercises, for example.

Webtours

These allow the presenter to take all participants to a particular website, which will open on their website. This can be helpful for demonstrations.

Recording

Some programs allow the meeting to be recorded. This is particularly helpful for those who were unable to attend.

▶ Practical considerations

Training

If you are new to online workshops you could practise with a colleague. Similarly, your participants may be new to the experience. Send out a list of preparations you want them to complete beforehand, such as making sure they have a microphone, tips on how to interact in an online class, and so on. Most programs allow participants to test their audio and video connections beforehand.

IT support

Depending on who organises the workshop, there may or may not be online IT support available. If there is, take advantage of it to test all aspects of the workshop beforehand. Are the audio and video clear? Can the other person see your Powerpoint presentation? If you plan to use virtual breakout rooms (see below), do they work?

Clear rules

Because the medium of online workshops is new for many participants, it is probably a good idea to establish some expectations. This can include how and when you would like participants to post questions (see below) and what type and amount of interaction is required (some participants could assume that because the workshop is online they will not have to contribute).

Proper preparation

As with face-to-face workshops, online meetings require good preparation on the presenter's part. In particular, have all the links you want to share ready, perhaps in Notepad or a similar application, so that when the time comes to visit the sites, you can simply copy and paste the relevant link, rather than having to type it in (which, in front a of an audience, can easily go wrong!).

Similarly, if you are using polls or quizzes, most programs allow you to create them beforehand so that when the time comes you can simply share them with the participants.

The same applies to documents or other files you want to share. Have these all in one place, for example on your desktop or in the same folder, where you can easily find and share them.

Timing

It may seem obvious, but online workshops conducted across different time zones mean that participants need to check when the event takes place for them. Common practice is to use the time zone of the host institution and use that *in all communication about the event*. This avoids confusion. For example, let's say that a company in London hosts an event for its staff in the UK, New York and India; the event would be advertised as taking place at 13:00 GMT. It is then up to participants to figure out what time that is in their own time zone (using, for example, www.timezoneconverter.com). Be careful that an event that is held on one day in a particular time zone may well be on a different day for participants in a different time zone. For example, one of us teaches at a University in California and classes are normally held at 17:00 on a Friday California time, which is 13:00 on Saturday in New Zealand. There is one extra trap when one of the countries turns its clocks forward and back twice yearly. Ask beforehand!

▶ Pedagogical considerations

Next we look at some of the specific pedagogical opportunities and challenges of delivering online workshops.

The basics

Many experienced workshop facilitators seem to forget most of what they know when they initially start presenting online, perhaps because there is so much to think about at the technical level. Consider your normal routine and make sure that you find a way to implement it in the online environment. For example, if you normally make it a habit to greet each participant as they come into the room, do the same in the chatroom as participants arrive, by being online a few minutes early and typing something like 'welcome <name>'. Similarly, if you usually like to schedule breaks every hour, continue to do so online. Tell people in how many minutes' time you would like them back (rather than mention a time, as participants may be in different time zones from you). In other words: don't forget basic, sound pedagogical practice.

Backchannelling: synchronous feedback from participants

One advantage of online workshops is that most programs have some way for participants to feed back to the presenter. Usually there is a chatroom where participants can post questions or comments, either to the presenter, to other participants, or to all. Make it clear from the start whether you will be monitoring the chatroom. Many presenters report that, over time, they come to appreciate this informal type of interaction, which allows them to keep a 'finger on the pulse' of the group. Participants enjoy being able to post questions without having to disrupt the group (as in a face-to-face situation), and other participants can sometimes answer questions as well. This type of interaction is called 'backchannelling', and although the number and the timing of the messages can be a bit overwhelming for those new to online interaction, it provides valuable insight into those areas that participants find enjoyable, difficult, or that they would like to learn more about. If you find it difficult to monitor contributions yourself, you could ask a colleague or participant to do this and alert you to problems.

Quizzes and polls

An extension of the backchannelling idea above, is to disseminate questions that participants can answer online. Depending on the functionality of the software, these can include simple yes/no questions, multiple choice, and a host of other question types. Most programs that include this functionality will also allow you to share the results with the group. Some facilitators use this to check understanding ('How well do you now understand X?'), to decide what to do next ('Would you like to hear more or move on to the next topic?') or for overall feedback on the workshop ('How helpful was this workshop for you?'). More extensive quizzes can also be created, to provide a more detailed check of understanding, for example.

Giving participants the floor

In addition, most programs allow you to make participants the 'presenter' in the same way as if they were coming to the front of the room to report the results of a group discussion. This means that their audio and video can be heard and seen by the other presenters.

Participant-to-participant interaction

Chatrooms allow participants to choose whether to post comments that are visible to all, or only to specific participants. This is an excellent way for participants to exchange information or ask questions without disrupting the rest of the group. Some facilitators pair participants at the start, for this purpose.

Virtual breakout rooms

Some programs allow presenters to allocate participants to particular groups, just as in face-to-face workshops. Different groups can be given different materials to work with (through 'file sharing'). This can be helpful for tasks that require participants to work on 'information gap' activities (see p. 160), for example. Groups of participants can be sent to different virtual breakout rooms. This means that each group can (at that point) only see its own participants, shares one chatroom, and can work with a shared set of materials. For workshop facilitators, virtual breakout rooms offer a wonderful opportunity to have different participants work on different activities together. When tasks are finished, everyone can return to the main room and a spokesperson could be asked to report their findings. As the presenter, you can move from breakout room to breakout room, and the comments you make in one room are only visible to participants in that room.

The use of breakout rooms can be challenging as you will need to juggle a lot of different tasks (just as in a face-to-face situation): create breakout rooms, assign participants to groups, send different materials to different groups, visit the groups and respond to comments, move around, end the group meetings, and so on. Clearly, this requires some familiarity with the software and it is recommended that you practise this beforehand.

Bring in guest speakers

As we mentioned, one advantage of an online workshop is that it is possible to bring in guest speakers for brief appearances. One of us regularly uses this as a way to have colleagues from different countries contribute something in their area of expertise. This can be for as little as a few minutes. Participants usually really appreciate these multiple perspectives.

Pre- and post-workshop tasks

It is relatively easy to post materials online for participants to use before the actual workshop. This could include reading materials, but also surveys that will help them to reflect on the subject and give you insight into their level of knowledge. Another option is to have participants use their webcams to record a brief welcome message to other participants.

As mentioned above, programs that allow you to record the interaction during the workshop make it easy to share materials with the participants afterwards. Depending on the nature of the workshop, you could include follow-up tasks and ask participants to share their experiences in implementing what they learned from the workshop.

Start easy

If you are new to online teaching, you may want your first experience to be a presentation rather than a workshop, as there is less interaction to handle. Once you feel comfortable, you could do a short workshop with a smaller number of participants, and easy tasks, before moving on to larger groups with multiple breakout rooms. As with all types of workshop, asking a colleague to sit in and give feedback afterwards is always a good idea.

> **YOUR TURN**
>
> Can you think of situations in your own job where an online workshop might be preferable?

▶ Software for presenting workshops online

Adobe Connect: paid software that includes many features, including the ability to create breakout rooms, polls, quizzes etc.

Gotomeeting: both paid and free versions. It includes the ability to create polls.

Google Hangout: free. Participants can share documents, see each other's videos, and you can record the meeting, but it does not include more advanced functionality.

For a comprehensive list of software with reviews, we recommend Jane Hart's website: http://c4lpt.co.uk/ – click on the link to the directory of learning performance tools and then the category web-meeting, conferencing and virtual classroom tools.

Professional development for facilitators

Although for most forms of teaching it is taken for granted that people are trained before starting, and then provided with ongoing professional development, this seems not always to be the case for those who lead workshops. Yet leading a workshop is very different from teaching a regular class and from giving talks in various places. Just as teachers can belong to a 'community of practice', so can workshop presenters. A number of options are open for workshop presenters to develop their skills and we will discuss this below.

For presenters who work in an institution that sends them out, their initial training and their ongoing professional development are most likely to be the responsibility of that institution. Do enquire about opportunities for initial training, and also ongoing supervision and any possible mentoring schemes that might exist. For freelance presenters there are options for formal study as well as a range of informal options.

Further study

Workshop presenters can further develop themselves in the area of their expertise in which they present their workshops, or in the area of teaching. As well as face-to-face courses, many institutions now also offer online opportunities. Decide how much time you want to commit to this, and whether you are available for on-site sessions once or twice a year if these are offered.

Tertiary providers Many tertiary institutions have in-house professional development programmes to which others can buy in. We are thinking here of mainstream, often government-supported places. When you are applying for a place on such a course, you could indicate areas where you would like training as well as mentioning your own strengths and contexts. This would help organisers put you in the right group or level.

Private training groups By contrast there are other, often more expensive, private institutions which offer specialised training on demand.

Online training/Distance learning providers Online training can be convenient, and has the added benefit of allowing you to learn through a medium that you will then be able to use in your own future teaching. As more workshops are delivered online (see the section on 'Delivering workshops online', p. 123), this will be a helpful skill to have.

In-house training In this case an institution draws on specific skills within its ranks. It can even be that there is no overall 'expert', but participants each offer to teach an area where they know more than others.

Training exchanges Sometimes institutions will set up an exchange system whereby someone from one place travels elsewhere to run a workshop, and then there is a reciprocal arrangement. This has the advantage of not costing anyone anything.

What learning takes place?

Skibba (2013) reports on research into the way faculty members (tertiary teachers) learn to teach in a new way. Although the context she describes is online course delivery, it seems her findings could be equally interesting to people learning to teach in workshops for the first time. Building on her ideas, we now suggest what a course (perhaps even a workshop) on professional development for presenters might look like. We consider two questions:

1 What do presenters need to understand?
2 How might a workshop contribute to that understanding?

In Table 2.13 we link suggested course content with suggestions for training presenters in this aspect.

Table 2.13 Training content and methods for workshop presenters

Content	Training suggestions
The place of technology	Offer options, to cater for all kinds of learners: Demonstration then practice Practice with one-to-one feedback (trial and error) Reading a manual before experimenting.
Experiential learning	Try out a range of learning activities for many different workshop topics. Create other activities for participants' own topics.
Learner-centred teaching	Observe and analyse video clips of workshops. Role-play specific situations such as giving clear instructions.
Social aspects of learning	Read and discuss case studies. Interview one another about experiences as workshop participants.
Workshop design	Compare a range of sample workshop timetables. Suggest modifications for particular contexts.

Table 2.13 summarises aspects of training. Without suggesting the complete content of a training event, here are some topics that are often covered in courses that prepare workshop presenters:

The place of technology It's a cliché to say that this is an ever-changing area. When Powerpoint first emerged there were workshops everywhere, advising presenters on its effective use. Now a technology workshop would include topics like 'using social media' or 'supporting mobile learning'.

Experiential learning Of the areas most frequently spoken of in adult learning, experiential learning (see the section on 'Adults as experiential learners', p. 53) is one that applies particularly to workshops. Whatever the topic, ideally participants should be able to experience the new learning. This applies as much to the trainers (workshop presenters) as to the learners (workshop attenders). When choosing a training mode, look at the small print to see what practical experience is offered. The experience could consist of having someone come to observe your next workshop to give you feedback on it. One other way of drawing on experience can be through being given a chance to report on your experience to date. Come to the training event prepared with some samples of your workshop timetables, handouts and realia.

Learner-centred teaching Workshops give a more active role to the learner and a more facilitative, rather than transmissive, role to the teacher. For many experienced teachers this transition can be challenging. Classes on learner-centred teaching deal with such topics as 'catering to diverse needs', 'alternative forms of assessment', 'developing learner autonomy' and so on. Before attending training on this subject, consider specific challenges you would face in your own work environment through changing to a more learner-centred teaching format.

Social aspects of learning This part of a course can deal with topics ranging from the affective to the organisational. People can be reminded that much learning is done in groups, with people whose views one appreciates. The topic can lead to practical applications such as ways of organising group work, as well as the ways in which technology can support (social) learning beyond the classroom.

Workshop design This is a more specialised topic. It teaches people how to plan their workshops, how to sequence activities, and how to monitor progress and assess learning. As we noted in Table 2.13, the training could include sample timetables, which can be analysed and used as templates for different topics.

Informal study

Apart from these formal courses, we recommend the following informal options:

attending other workshops	communities of practice
leader support groups	teaching portfolios
analysing critical incidents	case analysis
mentoring	team teaching
professional reading	action research
peer observation and evaluation	feedback from workshop participants

We now consider each of these in detail.

Attending other workshops

Simply attending workshops run by other presenters can be a help for collecting new ideas, both to imitate and to avoid.

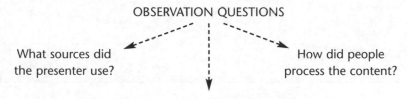

OBSERVATION QUESTIONS

What sources did   How did people
the presenter use?   process the content?

How were new ideas presented?

More specifically, you could design an observation form like Table 2.14, which helps you consider the advantages and disadvantages of each of the ways of presenting new content in a workshop.

Leader support groups

If you are part of an institution or workplace which regularly runs workshops, then having support meetings from time to time with other presenters can be a collegial form of professional development. People need not be from the same interest area. In fact, if they are not, then the talk can focus on organisational aspects. Coming to the group with a combination of concerns and triumphs can help start the ball rolling. For example:

'What do you do when ...?'

'Has anyone had the experience of ...?'

'I tried out one idea recently for ...'

Table 2.14 Observing workshops

Activity	Advantages	Drawbacks
Discussing case studies		
Matching terms and definitions		
Watching a demonstration		
Peer practice in small groups		
Planning ways to apply theory		
Responding to quotes, statements etc.		
Predicting outcomes		
Examples that come from participants' personal experiences		
Direct input through talk and Powerpoint		

Of course, people can keep in email contact between meetings, but face-to-face discussions can work even better because of the number of views. Having a firm chairperson will keep things moving.

Teaching portfolios

Some presenters build up a portfolio which helps them look at their development over time. This could include:

Participant evaluations
Handouts
Annotated notes made by you at the end of a session
Samples of participants' work.

Analysing critical incidents

We have mentioned critical incidents elsewhere (pp. 65–6), but here they are worth repeating as they can give considerable insight into the reasons why certain workshop practices did or did not work in a particular context. One way of using such incidents is to share them with colleagues and to ask for help in identifying triggers or causes that led to the specific outcome of the incident. What could have been done better, or differently?

Start by listing incidents from recent workshops that you'd like to revisit. Here are some suggestions. Think of occasions when:

You changed your plan
You didn't change your plan but later wished you had
A few attenders made things difficult
The organisers failed to prepare the venue as they had promised
You ran out of materials
You ran out of time.

Jot down all the details you can recall about these incidents and then prepare to have a chat with one or more other presenters. This could form a discussion point for your support group, mentioned above.

Case analysis

As with critical incidents, case analysis can be a good starting point for personal or collaborative reflection. Cases usually involve a more thorough look at a wider range of aspects of a workshop. For example, an organisation that has received particularly poor or particularly positive feedback on a workshop (or workshop series) may want to find out more about the reasons for this. Case analysis involves looking at the workshop from multiple angles: the facilitator's, the students', the administrators', the IT support team's, and so on. Case analysis involves asking questions that probe deeper than an average evaluation. For example, in addition to asking 'Did participants like the workshop?' a follow-up question might be 'Why did they (not) like it?' or 'Which parts were they enthusiastic about and which were they critical of?' and if the answer to that is found to be 'because the content was of the wrong level', then at least one further question is asked: 'What was wrong with it and how could it be improved?'

Mentoring

Choosing to mentor another, newer workshop presenter can be helpful in both directions. Sometimes, hearing the other person's experiences is like looking in the mirror. Although there is often an assumption that a more senior person will do all of the mentoring, fresh ideas or new insights from a junior presenter can be helpful for both parties. Choosing a mentor requires some consideration. You will want someone who is careful and constructive with their criticism. Similarly, when deciding to mentor someone else, be aware of their feelings. Always look for something positive to build on, and give specific examples relating to actual teaching practice. Focus on the practice, not the person. Also bear in mind that a good mentor plays different roles at different times, depending on what the presenter needs: instructor, critic, counsellor, listener, admirer.

Team teaching

As noted before, team teaching can have its advantages, and it probably goes without saying that you choose as your teaching partner someone you feel comfortable with, including being willing to accept their criticism. The experience of working and learning together can be particularly fruitful and allows both of you to draw on each other's strengths.

Professional reading

Reading professional journals in your field, and in the area of adult teaching and learning, is another way of keeping up to date. Your institution probably subscribes to some.

Action research

'Action research refers to teacher-conducted classroom research that seeks to clarify and resolve practical teaching issues and problems.' (Richards and Farrell, 2005: 171)

'AR is the superordinate term for a set of approaches to research which, at the same time, systematically investigate a given social situation ...' (Burns, 2010: 80–1)

As these two quotes illustrate, action research is usually thought of as happening for full-time teachers, but it can work too for people who frequently present workshops. Here are some steps, based on an actual example.

Step 1: Identify a problem
One presenter wanted to improve her spontaneous explanations when people asked her questions in the middle of a workshop.

Step 2: Plan a research method
She taped herself explaining points each time a student asked a question.

Step 3: Analyse the results
She and a colleague then listened critically to the results, identifying her responses and investigating their range. Next, they discussed alternatives and conducted a mini role-play around them.

YOUR TURN

What issues or problems would you like to investigate in your own workshop preparation and management?

(a) Plan a question/questions you could ask.
(b) How would you find answers?

Peer observation and evaluation

Having an honest peer come and give you feedback can be an easy and fairly quick way of measuring your own progress as a workshop presenter. Of course, being the one who observes someone else can also be helpful. If you are going for this path, think afterwards about the comments you write or give orally.

You try:

In Table 2.15 there are some sample comments made by peer observers. Consider how helpful you might find each of them.

Table 2.15 Sample comments

Comment	How helpful?
Directions for the activities seemed clear. The attenders seem to understand.	
You asked a lot of questions.	
You talk a little fast.	
I noticed people were paying attention the whole time.	
Watch out for spelling mistakes on your Powerpoint.	
Transitions between activities were good. No fumbling around.	
You were able to get them talking.	
Good communication.	

Sometimes you might want to guide the observer to look for particular points you are concerned about. For example:

'Do I talk too much?'

'What did you think of my response to wrong answers?'

Feedback from workshop participants

We deal with evaluation elsewhere (p. 216), but it is worth pointing out that the feedback you receive from participants can be a great source of information. Although not always comfortable to read, less-than-positive feedback can be very helpful to identify areas for improvement.

A suggestion to new workshop presenters would be to have a friendly supporter with you when you read your first feedback. Not everything that is written down may be worth worrying about!

Communities of practice

Communities of professionals in similar areas tend to emerge organically and can be a great source of support. Look beyond your institution or company, including online. Most have occasional meetings or online forums for participants to post questions and receive feedback.

PART 3
The practice of facilitating workshops

The 'when' of workshops

'The last time I offered a workshop it was on a Friday afternoon. The feed-back from the participants was that they were too tired and would have preferred it on another day. This time I gave the workshop on a Monday but now participants said they were too worried about all the week's tasks ahead. Is there a right time for workshops?'

The short answer to the above question is 'no'. It is unlikely that you will be able to satisfy all participants, most of whom will have different schedules and preferences. Nonetheless, there are some general considerations that will increase the likelihood of the workshop being at a convenient time for most.

- Enquire with the organisers about particularly busy periods at work for participants. Organising a workshop the day before a major deadline is not likely to be appreciated. However, in situations where participants come from a range of backgrounds, you may need to make a best guess. In general, the days before or immediately following major holidays are not ideal. Experience suggests that places of work record lower atten-dances on those days as people plan for a get-away.
- Much will depend on participants' reasons for attending. If participation is compulsory, and especially if it is assessed or counts towards some form of certification, the pressure on participants will be greater than if they choose to join out of personal interest. In the former case, participants may want more advance notice to prepare.
- If there is follow-up work for participants to complete after the workshop, ensure there is sufficient time to complete it. Avoid offering the workshop a few days before a holiday, for example.
- Another consideration is the time of day. If participants need to travel from far away, it may be better to start later in the morning. Workshops for parents with children at school may need to finish earlier.
- For workshops that are offered online (see the section on 'Delivering workshops online', p. 123), it is possible that participants are in different time zones. In this case, try to identify where the majority of your audi-ence comes from and choose a time that offers a suitable time for most. Use a website like www.timezoneconverter.com to find out the time in different time zones.

Timing issues

VIGNETTE

'The other day I was asked to do an introductory workshop for our human resources team on dealing with complaints. It is a very difficult topic and I normally spend at least a full day on it. The organisers, however, were adamant the workshop should last two hours maximum. I really struggled to make it a meaningful experience for the participants.'

Related to the issue of time is how long a workshop should be, or how short it can be. Of course, the key points of a workshop can be put on a handout and participants could read this themselves, but as we hope to have shown, the added value of workshops comes from the opportunities for interaction and gaining practical experience. Some organisers forget this important point and do not allocate enough time. If you feel this is the case, talk about it and perhaps share a brief outline of the activities (not just the content) you aim to complete with the participants, and the various (types of) learning outcomes (see the section on 'Writing goals, objectives and learning outcomes', p. 80) you are aiming for. The opposite can happen too. One of us was once asked to change a 2-hour workshop into a full-day event, supposedly because one of the other speakers cancelled. The workshop schedule was changed, with the morning dedicated to input and controlled practice, and the afternoon was used to have participants work in small groups based on their shared interests, with the facilitator walking around and giving feedback.

The length also depends on the audience. There is a big difference between the more leisurely pace of a workshop taken during employers' time and one for which people have to find their own time to attend. Evenings and weekends are the usual choice for people in the workforce, although for seniors and other groups free by day there is no reason why the atmosphere could not also be more leisurely.

If you cannot make the workshop as long as you think it should be, consider giving participants some tasks to complete beforehand. Participants could, for example, reflect on their current practice (in the example from the quote above, they could think about the way they responded to a complaint in the past), or bring sample documents or issues they would like to discuss. Also, you can extend the workshop (as suggested above) by giving participants tasks to complete afterwards, useful tools (such as observation sheets, checklists for self-assessment, sample scenarios, etc.), and by following up through email or by setting up a forum for participants to share experiences and to post questions.

Participant issues

▶ Determining your audience

A number of questions are raised by experienced workshops facilitators, and many of these start with questions about the audience.

Who selects the workshop participants?
Are there criteria set by the facilitator?
What happens if it becomes clear early in a workshop that one or two participants are in the wrong place?
How does a facilitator 'read' an audience as the workshop proceeds?
How feasible is it to adapt materials or methods to suit an unexpected audience?

Since many of these questions are interwoven, let's start with the experience of one of us. The anecdote is divided into three parts so that you can stop and ask yourself what you would have done under the circumstances.

VIGNETTE

Part 1
'I was invited to run a workshop in a different part of the country on a topic I was familiar with but by an organiser I had never met. This workshop would be part of a week-long conference at which a number of presenters would be running workshops, while others would give talks. There were also sessions where participants reported on their work experiences in various parts of the country.

About five minutes into the workshop, when people were about to break into small groups for a task, one woman spoke up.

"I didn't come to this conference to hear about ... This is a waste of time. I came to hear about ..." '

At this point in the anecdote, let's pause for a moment while you, the reader, consider what you might have done next. For example:

'I might have said ...'
'I might have done ...'

> ### VIGNETTE
>
> **Part 2**
> 'I turned to the conference organiser and suggested we have a short break for him to discuss with the participants what the majority would like to do. Meanwhile I would leave the room so they didn't feel inhibited. His answer was this.
>   "No. You're doing fine. Just carry on."'

Again, you might consider what you would have done next.

> ### VIGNETTE
>
> **Part 3**
> 'I then invited the woman who had interrupted, and any others who might feel the same, to leave and do something more useful to them. I emphasised that this would not cause any offence. The response from others was that they wanted to stay and learn from the session because it did seem relevant to them. The interrupter then said something along these lines:
>   "Oh well. I might as well just stay."'

One issue worth considering in this true account is the question of who is in charge at each point of an event. Clearly, before the presenter was introduced, proceedings were in the hands of the organiser. Usually the facilitator would be in charge during the workshop itself, but who is in charge if things go wrong? In this case there was more at stake than the content of the workshop. Since the host organisation had invested money into flying the presenter to the venue and then providing overnight accommodation, the option of simply dropping the workshop if it had seemed unsuitable to the majority of attenders would be a last resort.

Some planning can avoid a mismatch between the workshop content and the expectations of participants.

1 An abstract needs to be negotiated beforehand between the inviter and the invitee.
2 The negotiation involves more than the facilitator simply saying, 'This is what I'm doing.'
3 For negotiation to happen there needs to be a reasonable lead time for email exchanges.

4 Once agreed on, the abstract needs to be available to participants before the session.

5 If a topic seems likely not to appeal to everyone at a conference, offering alternative sessions is a good idea. It seems better to have people complaining about wanting to go to everything than to have the opposite.

▶ How many participants is right?

QUESTION

'I'd be interested to hear what other people do when they've been told to prepare for a workshop of 20 people but when the time comes there are twice that number clamouring at the door. Whose responsibility is it to turn people away?'

Organisers often ask ahead of time how many participants one is willing to accept into a workshop. Having given an answer, don't be surprised to arrive to find more, as this presenter reports.

VIGNETTE

'They had told me beforehand to expect 25 participants as this was the number that the room would hold. It became clear near the start that many more wanted to attend. I really didn't mind although they had to share resources, but it can't have been comfortable for them sitting on the floor and standing at the back.

A couple of years later I met someone who'd attended my workshop and I was expecting to hear a complaint. Instead, this person reported how much people had appreciated that I didn't make a fuss but just did my best to move around the room as they worked at activities. That was a relief. Maybe what some people take from a workshop is less the actual content and more about how to organise similar events themselves.'

The presenter above doesn't report why the numbers were so many more than predicted, but often there are reasons beyond the powers of the organisers to predict, such as the cancelling of other workshops for a variety of reasons, or the great, but unpredicted, popularity of one person.

You have, of course, the right to turn people away, but in that case you may simply be passing the problem on to another presenter. It is up to you to decide whether to stick to the agreed numbers or try to make the experience worthwhile for everyone.

If you do find yourself suddenly facing more participants than you expected, here are some suggestions. Here we assume that safety or specialist equipment are not issues.

1 Don't take complete ownership of the problem. Offer alternatives such as being willing to repeat the workshop that afternoon in a different conference slot. Go with whatever they suggest.
2 Ask if anyone would like to go and photocopy extra handouts or whether they are happy sharing.
3 Suggest that during group time some groups move into another area.
4 Offer a longer time for the tasks.
5 Have groups reporting back to some groups only, not to the whole audience.
6 Consider changing some of your activities to those that can be more easily handled with larger groups (see the section on 'Workshop activities', p. 93).

▶ Too many or too few participants

When the details of a workshop are being organised ahead of time, the number of attenders is one of the topics to be addressed. Apart from the obvious constraints of room size, and the need to run off enough handouts, both of which are usually the responsibility of the local organiser, what difference to the presenter do numbers make? We suggest that it can have an effect on both the process and the content.

Large numbers need not stop the typical processes of pair and small-group tasks, provided there is room for people to move around. Here are some suggestions.

1 Break into special interest sections for group work. These can be suggested by the facilitator and can be based on:

   ▶ years of experience
   ▶ workplace responsibilities
   ▶ preference for dealing with printed or audio or visual input
   ▶ mixing people who know each other and who are unfamiliar to one another.

2 Limit the report-back time each group is given.

What is *not* helpful is for the facilitator to say something like, 'Sorry, we've run out of time so we can't hear from the rest of you.' Experience soon lets a facilitator know ahead of time how long it will take to hear from each group. This can be conveyed to the groups ahead of time.

The opposite situation can also happen, although this may be more embarrassing to the organiser than to the presenter. The main disadvantages are:

▶ There may have to be only one group instead of several.
▶ Participants miss out on a range of experience from other participants.
▶ The workshop may finish sooner than planned.

There is nothing to be done at the last minute about this problem, but at least the presenter can make the experience worthwhile for those who do arrive. It is also tactful to avoid blaming the poor organiser, who is probably already feeling upset.

▶ **Handling signs of boredom**

QUESTION

'Sometimes I see people yawning, or even falling asleep. It always really unsettles me. I immediately think I must be a terrible presenter. Do others feel like this too?'

Ideally, you have thought beforehand about boredom and have planned for interest through variety, relevance of examples, breaks. However, if the situation does arise where someone loses interest, ask whether anyone else is concerned about this task. If others are also concerned, stop and explain briefly to everyone the purpose of the exercise/task they are working through and why, in the long run, doing the task will be more useful than being told the 'answers'.

If nobody else is concerned, invite the speaker to chat about it with you one-to-one.

Seeing someone yawn or look bored does not necessarily mean they find the workshop uninteresting. One of us had the experience of an audience member at the front of the room falling asleep but coming up to the front during a break to apologise, saying that she had been looking after a sick relative but was enjoying the workshop very much.

▶ Different types of participants

QUESTION

'The range of people I've seen in workshops is staggering. How do presenters deal with such diversity?'

We usually assume that workshops attract people who are interested in the advertised topic (although, as we have seen, that is not always the case), but even assuming they are all interested, what hitches can you expect to meet at your workshop? Experience suggests that knowing ahead of time the range of responses people will have to your workshop makes you better able to deal with tricky situations. In this section we draw on our, and other people's, experiences as the starting point for making suggestions for working helpfully with some common workshop 'types'.

(A) *I thought this workshop was going to be about … not …*

There are two common causes of mismatches between the attenders and the topic.

1 Wrong room
   If your workshop is part of a bigger event such as a conference, perhaps there has been a mistake and the person has walked into the wrong room.
      Particularly at large events with other sessions, start your workshop with a quick announcement of the topic. Make it clear that this is what is on the conference programme.
2 Unclear publicity
   Sometimes the publicity has not made the content perfectly clear. Run your proposed publicity blurb past someone in the targeted group. Ask them to tell you in their own words what the workshop topic will be. Also, if the publicity is being sent out from some central point and others have contributed to it, ask to see all publicity about your workshop before it is sent out.

(B) *Stop wasting my time*

'Why are you making us play these games? Why don't you just tell us the answer? I have important work waiting for me back at my desk.'

These people want you to know how very busy they are. Unlike others who, they imply, are at the workshop to fill in time, they have no time for any activity which could take longer than reading a page of suggestions or listening to a ten-minute talk. Similarly they are intolerant of anything which they cannot immediately see is part of the topic.

What causes this problem?

1 Some people have been forced to come to the workshop
There are one or two possible responses here. If you can manage to do it without sounding sarcastic you could offer to send the person your Powerpoint summary so that they can leave the workshop and do something else.

2 Genuine misunderstanding about the nature of a workshop
An underlying problem can be that people have not been made aware of the difference between a talk/presentation and a workshop. In conference publicity, organisers sometimes provide definitions such as:

> 'The presenter sessions held in the main meeting room are designed as times for input, whereas the purpose of the workshops is to involve participants in different ways of learning.'

It can also be helpful to address these comments by saying something like this:

> 'People learn in different ways. During this workshop the intention is to provide opportunities for people who learn by doing and talking.'

Dealing with these and other types of workshop attenders

1 The wrong room

The complainant who came to the wrong topic needs to have the problem sorted out as quickly as possible. If others can keep working, then invite the person to check their conference programme and see whether perhaps they really have come in the wrong door. Once, when one of us had someone with this problem, we turned to the person chairing the workshop to see if he could sort things out. In that case the incident concluded with the woman saying, in an ungracious tone, 'Oh well. I might as well stay.' It took a few minutes for the frosty atmosphere to clear.

2 The interrupter

The second type of person needing tactful attention is the constant inter-rupter. This person starts swinging into action during the time when you are explaining the task. The interruptions may anticipate something you are just about to explain.

'Excuse me but you haven't told us how to choose our groups.'

'Are we going to have feedback time?'

'Do you want us to ... or to ...?'

Or the interruptions may come later, in the middle of another group's pres-entation. Some of these interruptions may be necessary.

'Do you mind speaking up?'

'Could you use the mike please? We can't hear a word you're saying.'

Other interruptions come from impatience.

'The last group has just said that.'

'Just a minute. That idea wouldn't work for us.'

POSSIBLE CAUSES OF THE PROBLEM

Forgetting their role. Some workshop topics attract attenders who are used to being in charge of groups. They forget that at this moment their role is not that of organiser.
A genuine problem, such as poor audibility or unclear instructions.
Centre-stage phenomenon. Some people really do find it hard not to be visible or audible in a group. These people come into their own at dinner parties, where they tend to dominate conversations, but unlike the dinner host, you have the right to do your own interrupting if things become too difficult for other attenders, not just you.

SUGGESTIONS

1 It is easy to be annoyed by interrupters, but staying calm helps the atmos-phere. Remember that if you are annoyed, then others are likely to be

annoyed too. They will be grateful if you can manage the interruptions in a firm but pleasant way.

2 Indicate if the problem is about to be addressed anyway.

'Thanks for that point. I thought I'd explain ... before coming onto that.'

3 Invite others to say whether it's a problem for them as well.

'Is anyone else finding it difficult to read the board?'

4 Move on fairly quickly. If the person is trying to interrupt one of the report-backs, try saying:

'Good point, but shall we hear them out first and then take additional ideas?'

3 The overtalker

Some participants simply talk too much. What they have to say may be interesting and relevant and even acceptable to other participants, at least for the first five minutes.

POSSIBLE CAUSES

This person really does have a great deal of information worth sharing.
The speaker prefers speaking, to listening.
The person's usual job involves an up-front role.

SOME SOLUTIONS

Try walking towards the speaker while looking interested. Then when the moment is right, say something like 'Thanks'. That often works.
If not, try the next step.
Interrupt with something constructive:

'It strikes me that you have some experience that a lot of people would be interested in. Would you be willing to lead one of the discussion groups after the break?'

4 The silent one

Then there is the opposite problem. Some workshop participants never actually speak, although the sad thing is that often nobody notices this silence. If we believe that learning new ideas and skills includes processing them, then the workshop presenter can be on the lookout for this silent person.

Causes	Possible solutions
Some people genuinely prefer to learn by listening and watching.	Not all activities need to be in small groups. Try giving some pair work.
The content may be so far above someone's head that they really have nothing to say.	Move around the room noticing any people who are not contributing. Try to engage them in conversation naturally when there is a chance, such as asking a question that is not too challenging. 'Are you finding that some of this relates to your experience?' 'Will you be able to use any of these skills in the future?'
Shyness.	Bring the problem into the open before the next group time by suggesting the people appoint a group leader, one of whose roles is to encourage everyone to contribute.
English (or whatever is the language of the workshop) may be the person's second language.	In a genuinely mixed linguistic group, invite people to work with others of the same language for just some of the activities
Very occasionally there is a physical reason, such as a stammer, which stops someone from speaking up in a group of strangers.	Talk to the participant beforehand or during a break, to ask them if they would like to contribute publicly or would prefer not to.
Someone may be waiting for a chance to speak but is never called on, even in a small group.	Check that you invite all participants to contribute.

5 The fast finisher

Some fast finishers choose to keep talking in their little groups and see it as a chance to chat about other things, but for the workshop organisers it's those who announce their early finishes that call for a response.

'What should we do when we've finished?'

'That was easy. It didn't take us long.'

CAUSES

A wide range of experience in the workshop.
The group have actually skipped several steps of the instructions.
It took the presenter so long to hand out the materials that some groups were halfway through before others could start.

POSSIBLE SOLUTIONS

Having some individuals finishing faster than others is inevitable in group work. Be ready for it. One way to avoid the staggered starting times is to have all the materials out on a table and to invite a representative from each group to come and help themselves to one pile.
Fast finishers can sometime come to the front and start writing up the key words for their report back.
Ask other groups, particularly those that are struggling, whether they'd like someone new to join their group and add ideas.
Go and chat with the early finishing group to see that they really have covered everything you intended.

6 I must stay with my friends

This problem refers to grouping arrangements. As we will see later, there are many ways of forming groups: optional group / numbered off grouping; different interests / same interests; friends / strangers. But beware! Some people don't want to move away from the people they came with.

CAUSES

Social reasons For many people the social side of the workshop can overtake the other purposes.

Comfort zones For other people new situations are challenging or even frightening. Although having come to the event to learn new ideas, they do not think that meeting new people should be part of that.

Laziness Perhaps their friends are the ones sitting closest to them when the instruction comes to 'form groups'.

POSSIBLE SOLUTIONS

Explain the purpose of whichever form of grouping you think would be most useful for this topic.

'The point of working with people from another workplace is so that we can collect examples of different practices.'

Make a joke of it.

'I know you all like your friends but …'

Invite participants to nominate the type of grouping they'd like for the next activity.

7 The off-taskers

When you move around the room you may notice that some people are completely off task.

POSSIBLE CAUSES

Your instructions were unclear.
The task is too difficult.

SOME SOLUTIONS

Some task instructions are better written down on the board, a Powerpoint or cards for each group.

8 The adviser

The adviser usually approaches the workshop facilitator over morning tea or another break. This person has a number of suggestions for you.

'You're doing well, but I think it might help if you …'

'Have you noticed how many people aren't taking any notes. Why don't you …'

'Have you considered ...'

'On the last workshop I attended, the presenter ... That worked well.'

'You might like to know that some people are wishing ...'

POSSIBLE CAUSES

There really is a problem.
The speaker wants to show solidarity with the presenter.
Others have asked this person to make the suggestion.

SOME SUGGESTIONS

First, try to keep calm. However helpful the advice might be, it's not always easy to take suggestions when you have spent days preparing for the event.
Say that you'll consider that idea. Then go and ask for advice from one of the organisers or even from another participant. Their responses will guide you as to whether to take action.
Say that you'll keep that idea in mind for the next workshop but now that all the materials are prepared you can't change things this time.

9 What are you doing tonight?

Here we come to a delicate topic, namely the out-of-hours relationship between workshop presenters and attenders. Although some would say that adults, unlike participants, can form whatever liaisons they like in their spare time, in the case where a workshop continues to the next day, the atmosphere can be affected if an individual in the group and the presenter have some kind of bonding that excludes others.

CAUSES

A group of adults find themselves in a new setting with none of their usual after-hours responsibilities.
The presenter, being in a position of power, comes across as more glamorous than usual.
The presenter (or the person the presenter has approached) is flattered at the attention.

POSSIBLE SOLUTIONS

Everyone will have an opinion on this one, but a rule of thumb is that if your role is facilitating a workshop for a number of people, then anything that could spoil the effective conclusion of the workshop is worth avoiding. The person who makes the first move is sometimes a participant and sometimes the presenter, but generally it's the latter who has the responsibility for the smooth running of the event. Of course, once the workshop is over, adults will do whatever they want to do.

You may wonder, after reading this section, whether workshops are just one long headache. Not at all. You will meet the willing contributors, the witty interjectors, the thoughtful contributors. It's just that you don't need advice on how to work with them, and therefore descriptions of them would have made boring reading.

To be fair, there are also ways in which a presenter can irritate attenders, but let's leave that for another section.

▶ Great diversity of participant needs and interests

In any given workshop you are likely to find participants with vastly different needs and interests. Catering to everyone in the room is one of the major challenges that facilitators face. Some workshops are offered to relatively homogeneous groups (for example, everyone from the same office) but in many cases workshops are advertised widely and you may find participants from different professional fields, with different levels of knowledge and experience, and with very different reasons for attending. Here is a breakdown of a recent workshop (on 'self-access in teaching') one of us gave at a university in Singapore.

Total number of participants		21
Professional background	Academic	9
	science	4
	arts	2
	humanities	3
	Government	5
	Business	7
Experience with the subject	A lot	4
	Some	4
	Little	7
	None	6

Attendance	Compulsory	
	paid	12
	unpaid	1
	Voluntary	
	paid	3
	unpaid	5

Even the above does not do justice to the diversity in this group. For example, some of the government staff worked as assessors, and others as policy makers. Participants' ages ranged from 19 to 68. Some were junior staff, some middle management, and some leaders in their institutions. How can we deal with such diversity?

If you know beforehand (or expect) that your audience will be diverse, you can take this into account in several ways. A good first step is to look at the *learner differences* below, and identify where you expect the greatest divergence as well as their impact on the workshop. The first one has been done as an example.

The next step is to focus on those differences that have a high impact and plan ahead to deal with these, using the tips below. Bear in mind that some differences can potentially have a high impact but may only affect a small number of participants. In such cases you may decide not to change the

Table 3.1 Learner differences

Learner difference	Comments	Impact (high or low)
Attendance	Some participants are required to take this Saturday morning course. They may be resistant.	High
Motivation		
Age		
Previous experience with the subject		
Length of experience in the profession		
Extravert or introvert		
Beliefs		
Anxiety		

content of your workshop but instead to use one of the options further down.

Flexible syllabus design

In the section on 'Sequencing content and activities' (p. 117) we described different types of syllabus design and ways of sequencing content. To cater for diversity, a modular or matrix model may be more suitable than a linear or spiral model, as you will have greater flexibility in deciding what to cover next, depending on participants' level, interests and progress.

Differentiation

The above are all ways of building flexibility into the curriculum, but all participants essentially cover the same content. There are, of course, situations where that is not preferable, for example when the differences in learners' needs are too great. In such cases, you may want to use one of the following techniques:

▶ Allocate participants to different groups. It may not be possible to provide each group with completely different information (as you would essentially end up running two or more workshops concurrently!), but different groups could look at the same topic from different angles, for example.

▶ Use information-gap tasks. Participants hold different pieces of information and need to collaborate to complete an activity. You can provide different kinds of information to different participants – for example, commercial information to academics, and academic information to business people in the audience.

▶ Even when people have different levels of experience with a topic, they usually are happy to share their opinions. Opinion-gap tasks are useful for this.

▶ Provide additional reading materials as part of the activities. Participants who know a subject well may need less time to complete the activities. By including additional background reading or other materials, these participants have an opportunity to widen their knowledge.

▶ Include optional questions or mini-tasks for participants to complete individually. Where possible, you could go around the room and give feedback while slower participants are still completing their tasks.

▶ Allow participants to choose from different types of activities. You could, for example, offer a discussion activity (which will probably appeal more to vocal and extravert participants) and a self-assessment task, both of which would deal with the same subject.

▶ Use mini-projects. Project work allows different participants to take different roles. For example, less experienced members of a team could look up, or read about, previous solutions to a problem, and more experienced members could use this to design their own alternatives.

The reality is that it is often impossible to cater to everyone's needs in a group. If you fear that this will be the case, you could address this subject head on and explain that some aspects of the workshop may be rather familiar to some of the participants, and other aspects may be too advanced. Another way of acknowledging this issue is by providing participants with materials to take home, either for them to read up on some of the more advanced subjects, or to provide additional resources for the more advanced participants to extend their knowledge.

▶ Unwillingness to participate

Humility

Sometimes people say nothing because they feel intimidated by others, as this vignette shows.

VIGNETTE

'I have found that one thing that stops people from contributing in workshops is when I start by asking people, in turn round the room, to report on their interest in the topic. If some people indicate that they know a lot about something it immediately keeps others quiet.'

Language problems

Some participants are simply not used to speaking in front of groups. Don't force them. There's no reason why everyone should speak to the whole hall. Let them contribute in small groups.

Shyness

This can happen when most people seem to know one another and one person feels left out. Let people select their own groups but be on the look-out for someone who's left out and someone else who looks compassionate!

Lack of motivation

This is more difficult to deal with. As discussed in the section on 'Motivation' (p. 24), motivation is a multi-faceted concept, meaning that participants seldom come for just one reason. Similarly, they may be encouraged to participate, even if the workshop does not meet their expectations – for example, you could look for other ways to relate the content to their interests or their beliefs. In one case, one of us was successful in 'enlisting' some reluctant participants who felt they already knew the workshop content, by appealing to their desire to help and teach others. These participants ended up playing a very productive role in the workshop, and later admitted to learning a great deal in the process. The key is to find out what makes your participants 'tick', not only at a professional but also at a personal level. Small talk during breaks can be particularly useful for this.

Do not believe in group work

A common reason for participants not to contribute is that they do not enjoy group work. Of course, workshops usually involve a great deal of collaboration, but if you feel resistance, it may be possible to substitute some of the activities with pair or individual work. Another approach is to explain the rationale for the group activities, for example by emphasising different participants' different backgrounds and experiences.

Organisational issues

> ## QUESTION
>
> 'My problem is timing the breaks during the workshops. Sometimes the coordinator tells me ahead of time that we must have breaks at such and such a time because that's when the catering staff prepare food and drinks. When the time comes, at that very moment we could be in the middle of an activity. How do I handle that?'

Causes

Too many constraints beyond the control of the presenter
Inexperience in predicting the length of tasks
Inflexibility on the part of organisers.

Solutions

One suggestion is to negotiate the break times with the coordinator, but that's not always a solution. Whatever time you planned a break there would always be times when it was inconvenient to stop. Here are a few other solutions that have worked in workshops we have organised or attended.

One is to say that participants will boil the water themselves when they are ready. This takes two or three minutes away from the workshop time but most people are happy to chat while they wait. Another solution is to ask people to collect their refreshments and bring them back to eat and drink while they continue the task.

A third solution depends on predicting how things are going, and not starting a lengthy task just ten minutes before break time. Be ready with one or two small tasks which can be done at any time when there's a short amount of time to fill in. It also pays to have tasks which can be interrupted when a session is moving toward break time.

Often what people remember later is the atmosphere of the workshop. If the facilitator constantly looks anxious and keeps checking the time, or speaks fast to fit everything in, then the impression is one of anxiety and the learning won't be remembered as well as that impression. You may have planned for people to note ten points from the source they are examining, but eight at a calm pace may be more reasonable and even more memorable.

Many presenters use music to create a relaxing atmosphere during breaks, and often also before the workshop starts and as participants settle in. Some presenters leave some music on in the background and then slowly raise the volume to alert participants that it is time to finish their work. Regardless of its timing, the use of music has been shown to have a positive effect on learning outcomes (Dosseville, Laborde and Scelles, 2012).

▶ Closing

> ### QUESTION
>
> 'I'm never quite sure what to do at the end of the workshop to end it in the "right" way. The ending sometimes seems slightly awkward.'

The closing of the workshop is particularly important as it is an opportunity to review all of the content and to give people a chance to reflect. With every workshop, make sure you:

Go over the objectives with participants to make sure all have been met
Give participants an opportunity to feed back on the workshop, by explaining what they feel they have learned and what is 'next' for them
Recommend further practice and implementing of what they have learned
Hand out any materials for further reading, as well as practical information for participants on how they can contact you or one another.

Problem 1 *Leaving the room as you found it*

'I try never to buy into the condition that I am responsible for putting all the hall furniture back in the right place. It cuts time from the workshop and creates a messy ending. Some people feel they should help me while others (understandably) have appointments to go to. I never know how long to leave for the tidying up anyway.'

Causes
Several reasons can lead to this messy situation.

1 The group inviting you doesn't own the room.
2 The room has been let on the condition it is returned to the way it was set up. If not, the group will never get the room again.
3 The organisers are too busy to help.

Solution

The simplest solution is to do as the person suggested above and simply don't agree to take time from your workshop for this other role. It's one thing to offer to help when one person is struggling to move furniture at the end of the workshop, but it's another to see the task as your responsibility. You need to be clear about what time the workshop is to finish and how long people will need later, to clear up.

Problem 2 *Speeches*

'More than once I've found that after I finish on time, someone will leap up to make a speech of thanks and present me with something. While this is happening some people are looking quite restless. What can I do?'

The cause for this may be that the organiser has poor time keeping or has simply failed to predict that this almost always happens. There really is not much you can do except for keeping your own speech short!

Technical issues

QUESTION

'Do I need to use the latest software to give a good workshop? Sometimes I wonder if I am just being lazy not to keep up with all the latest technologies. How do I know what is worthwhile using in class?'

In answer to the question above, technology is only a tool. In certain situations it can help make good teaching better, but it cannot make bad teaching good. Broadly speaking, technology can help with the *creation* or the *delivery* of workshops and can be used for their *organisation* or *pedagogical* benefits. Below is a summary from Reinders and White (2010) of the main potential advantages of using technology for teaching.

Table 3.2 The affordances of technology

Organisational	
Access	Workshop could be delivered from anywhere to learners anywhere.
Storage and retrieval of learning behaviour records and outcomes	Less relevant in workshops than in classes that meet more frequently.
Sharing and recycling of materials	This refers not only to colleagues' materials but also to being able to re-use your own materials. In addition, participants' contributions could be used in future workshops. This could include recordable presentations, their forum posts, contributions to a wiki, and so on.
Cost efficiency	The use of open source materials could help with the production of workshops, and participants could complete some of the preparation work beforehand or practise further afterwards, with the help of (online) materials.
Pedagogical	
Authenticity	It is very easy to find, integrate and share authentic samples.
Interaction	Contributing in public can be intimidating and certain online tasks can increase participation. As we have noted more than once, participants can also be encouraged to continue to collaborate after the workshop ends.

Table 3.2 *continued*

Pedagogical *continued*	
Situated learning	Technology can be used to provide locally relevant information and support.
Multimedia	The ability to include audio and video materials in a workshop is a major advantage, especially as these materials can now be easily shared with the participants (where copyright allows), after the workshop, for further practice.
New types of activities	Workshop materials can include activities that are difficult or impossible to achieve using other learning materials, such as moving objects across the screen (matching), recording one's voice, etc.
Feedback	In addition to feedback from the presenter, websites and computer programs can give feedback to participants about certain tasks. This is particularly helpful for further practice after the workshop. Backchannelling (see below and p. 129) also allows participants to give feedback to the presenter during the workshop.
Non-linearity	Participants working individually can easily navigate through materials according to their specific needs and interests. Similarly, the presenter can select from a range of materials based on the needs of the group.
Monitoring and recording of learning behaviour and progress	Less applicable in most workshops than in class, this can nonetheless be helpful in situations where workshop attendance and a demonstration of learning are necessary for certification or funding.
Control	All the above give presenters and participants greater control over the ways they interact with the workshop content.

▶ Some useful tools

Below, we look at some practical tools that could be used for the delivery of workshop content. These are based on Reinders, Lewis and Kirkness (2010).

Presentation software

Presentation software like PowerPoint, Prezi and Keynote allows the integration of text, graphics, and audio and video. If used well, presentation software can help you structure the workshop content and present the information in a visual way. By spreading content out over different slides you can clearly separate different topics, just as with overhead projectors (OHTs).

If presentations are published online they provide a useful resource for participants. These can be designed to include notes, quizzes and tests, thus allowing participants further practice after the workshop. A potentially advantageous characteristic of presentation software is that the content can be altered on screen. Of course, text and drawings can be added to overhead projectors, but presentation software allows greater flexibility and more options. Participants can contribute ideas, work in groups and suggest changes, and the end result can be presented to all.

Creating good presentations takes skill. A number of points to be aware of are discussed below.

Putting your presentation together

▶ First decide if you need to use presentation software. If you are only going to read your text out loud, perhaps you can do without. It is much better to be a lively speaker facing the audience than a reader turning to the board or screen all the time. It will save you time.

▶ As with overheads, make sure you use large enough fonts. Eighteen point or larger is recommended.

▶ Keep the amount of information per slide limited. For example, there is plenty of information to read in one graph so it is better not to clutter your slide with two. But avoid chunking and abridging information to the point where it is no longer comprehensible.

▶ Most programs let you create different types of slide transitions, and all sorts of animations. Often these do not add much and can distract from the overall message. Of course, they can also be very useful. For example, if you are using progressive build-up and want to show complex diagrams, it can be a good idea to start with one or two parts and then have other parts appear with the click of the mouse so that participants can see how all the parts relate to each other. Or, by using animations, you can show how two or more parts are connected; an additional part can be attached from outside, for example when describing the building of a car, or a new part can appear within another part, for example when describing biological processes. In short, eliminate all special effects that don't add meaning to your message. You don't want to distract your audience.

▶ Be careful with colours and unnecessary graphics. Remember that what looks good on screen can look bad on paper. Black text on a white background is good for both modes but white text on a blue or black background is only good for on-screen display. Colours are better left for showing pictures or other visual information where they have added value.

▶ Remember the importance of white space.

▶ Sometimes it is not clear how one slide relates to the next – it is useful to show an overview of your presentation at the beginning, and to show it again when you move on to a new topic so that people can follow your talk.

▶ Use slide titles and possibly slide numbers so the participants can see what each slide is about. This is also helpful if they missed what you said earlier.

▶ Consider alternatives for PowerPoint and Keynote. Prezi, Emaze and other applications can offer interesting alternative ways of displaying content.

Delivery

▶ To read out or not to read out? Be careful not to just read everything out for the participants.

▶ Practise beforehand, and check that all the technical facilities are working. Preferably do this the day before.

▶ Try out the presentation on a colleague and invite comments. What may be clear to you may not be clear to others. You can use a laser pointer to point to a detail on the screen. Frequent presenters may wish to invest in an infrared remote control that can be used to move between slides from a distance; this is ideal for group work.

▶ Powerpoint does not have to be a passive tool, but it needs to be integrated carefully.

▶ Create a special slide, 'Now your turn', and insert it at regular intervals when participants are expected to do an activity.

▶ Even though the presentation may be in a certain order, try to be flexible. Don't hesitate to turn on a blank screen when you want the participants' attention or to move between slides. Use the B key to return to a blank screen in the middle of the presentation so that you can introduce interactive tasks for your participants. Pressing B again will take you back to where you were in the slide show.

▶ Change the slide content, for example by having participants suggest changes, or by creating content (e.g. a graph) based on classroom discussion.

A brief word on mindmapping software

Mindmapping software has been successfully used by presenters to demonstrate ideas and processes, and also to facilitate group discussion and incorporate student ideas into a visual image. Because ideas can be easily linked, new ideas added and changes made and represented visually, mindmaps offer the potential for interactive classroom work. The end result can be printed, emailed to participants, posted on a website or included in a Powerpoint presentation.

Backchannelling

Presenters can have a hard time knowing who has understood the explanation, who is engaged, and who is merely present. The larger the number of participants, the harder this job becomes and, especially where time is short, opportunities for inviting feedback and checking understanding are minimal. To deal with this, various backchannel technologies have been developed that allow presenters to request feedback, check understanding and monitor participation, and for participants to respond, with the answers becoming available to the presenter (or everyone in class), usually in the form of a chart or a percentage. Teachers can choose to display the answers on an overhead projector for all to see, or can look at them on a computer at the front of the class. Similarly, teachers can choose to respond online or by reading out a question or comment.

Feedback technologies come in different flavours. Until a few years ago they were mostly hardware based, using specially designed handheld 'clickers' and 'trackers' (these looked like mini remote controls) that connected to a local network to allow participants to answer 'yes' or 'no' to questions by pressing the appropriate button, and displaying the information through an overhead projector. With mobile phones and tablets becoming ubiquitous and connectivity improving, most solutions nowadays involve the use of participants' phones or laptops to do the same thing (this is sometimes referred to as BYOD, or 'Bring Your Own Device'). Participants log in to a website or start an app on their phone or tablet, post or answer questions and share these through SMS (text messages) or wifi.

There are many such programs and apps available, both free and paid for, but also general programs are often used, such as chat applications or Twitter. A chat window that all participants log in to (including the teacher) allows everyone to post and read comments. Twitter can be used in the same way, but to make it easier to find the relevant messages, best practice is to create a 'hashtag' that participants can use in their posts. (A hashtag is like a label starting with the symbol # that will allow people to contribute to a particular topic.) There are also programs that use Twitter but create closed environments that are visible only to particular people; ideal for use in class. The site twtpoll.com is an example.

Social networking

Many social networking sites can be used to create a community for participants. The advantage, especially for longer workshops where attenders do not know each other beforehand but will be working together for several days, is that they can introduce themselves and perhaps exchange their experiences before the start of the workshop. Similarly, sometimes such communities stay active and can share what they learned from the workshop, and their success in and questions about implementing this.

What next?

A good starting point to figure out what has worked for other teachers is to join in one of the many online forums on 'educational technology' and see how others have been able to make the technology work for them and their learners, not the other way around.

▶ When the technology fails you

Technology is a real help for workshop facilitators, but you can count on it failing – usually at the worst possible time, and not only when you travel to remote areas. There are ways of minimising the chances of this happening and the impact on your workshop if it does.

Ask questions beforehand

This doesn't always work, but having a list of questions that you send ahead in good time might help you predict some of the problems below.

Use common file formats

It is prudent to save documents and presentations in a format that can be read on as many different computers as possible. For example, if you use a later version of Microsoft Word, the default file format is [.docx]; however, your host institution may use an earlier version of the program, which only reads files saved as [.doc]. To save documents as .doc, click on the 'Home' button and then 'Save As' and select 'Word 97-2003 format'. An even safer option is to save files as .rtf (Rich Text Format), which can be read by many different programs. If you are ever on a computer that cannot read your files, try opening them from Google Drive, or use one of the many free available conversion tools (Google, free online file conversion programs).

Table 3.3 Dealing with technical issues

The presenter's computer (or projector) does not work	For all of the issues below, always try restarting the equipment first. Always bring your notes as printouts, and either have your presentations available as overheads, or include images of each screen in the handout (most presentation software lets you print out thumbnail pictures of all of your slides). You may also be able to use one of the participants' computers. In smaller groups you may be able to sit around a single computer, or if you have a laptop you can pass it round.
Participants' computers do not work	If you had planned activities for participants to complete on the computer, then this will require some on-your-feet thinking. If only some computers do not work, can the individual activities be done in pairs or small groups? Is it possible to schedule coffee breaks at different times? If all the computers fail, can some of the tasks be done with the handouts you prepared? For example, a task that requires participants to look up information from a specific website can be replaced with one where you hand out a one-page summary for discussion. If the presenter's computer does work, perhaps tasks can be done in a different format; you show the website and participants contribute as a group.
Internet connection problems	Firstly, if you are connecting through wifi, try connecting the computer using a LAN cable (and vice versa). It is useful to always carry a spare LAN cable. It is good to save screenshots of the websites you want to show, so that you have a backup. Also, always download copies of audio and video materials so that you can play them from the computer, rather than stream them. There is also software that lets you download websites for offline browsing. If the internet connection is too slow, see if you can pair or group participants to use a smaller number of computers. This may help. If it is vitally important that you access a live site, then open the sites you need before participants arrive. Even if this means negotiating different times for the transport arranged by your hosts.
Sites that don't work	Always have alternatives at hand, in case a site is down. If you just want participants to see what a site is like, you may be able to just show them your saved screenshots using the presenter computer and projector.

Unable to get the (overhead) projector to work	Many classrooms are set up with e-lecterns where different kinds of equipment share one projector, such as a TV screen, a DVD player, a computer, and an overhead projector. It is important to select the right 'input', also called a 'source'. Usually there is a button that lets you switch from one to the next, or there are dedicated buttons for each. Some systems are operated by touch screens on the computer. Also check the connection between the computer and the projector. There should be a VGA cable (a cable with 15 pins in 3 rows) going from the computer to the projector.
No sound over the speakers	See the previous entry. If you have selected the correct input, check (1) that the speakers do not need turning on manually (there may be an on/off or volume button on them), and (2) that the sound on the computer is on. You can do this by clicking the **Volume** icon in the System Tray (bottom of the screen) and adjusting the volume. By double-clicking on it (or by clicking **Settings > Control Panel > Sounds**) you can also adjust volume settings. Maybe the sound is muted.
The DVD player does not work	As a backup, it is always a good idea to 'rip' (copy) DVDs and CDs to your computer and carry them with you on a portable drive, in case the equipment fails.
Power failure	This is not at all uncommon in certain contexts. Participants will usually be able to tell you how long the power is likely to be out. You may be able to simply shift some activities around. In some places, power failures are more common at certain times of the day and it may be worthwhile planning your workshop to avoid those times. However, a thunderstorm can strike unexpectedly anywhere in the world. If the power is unlikely to come back on any time soon, you will be grateful for the hard copy backups you made earlier. Use handouts or printouts (for example, with reading materials) as sources for the activities. Give participants large paper and different coloured marker pens to brainstorm, create posters, and to report back to the rest of the class later. So-called butcher paper comes in rolls and has the advantage that you can tear off as much as you need. Props are useful too, in such situations. If you anticipate the possibility of a power failure, consider bringing in items that could serve as discussion points, for example. (See more on the topic of workshop tasks in the section 'Workshop activities', p. 93.)

Backing up

As anyone who has lost their workshop notes will recommend, always back up everything. USB sticks go missing, computers stop working and files become corrupt. Therefore you need at least three forms of backup:

Hard copies (see below)
Electronic copies on a computer, phone, or portable hard drive (e.g. a USB stick)
Online copies. You can email to yourself any files you need, or upload them to sites like Dropbox, or create them directly online on sites like Google Drive'

Check out the facilities

Where practically possible, it is a good idea to check out the facilities before your workshop. If you cannot, try to ask someone to do the steps below for you.

▶ If you will be using the host institution's computers, check that they can open the files you will use (both presenter and participant computers). Are the computers particularly slow to start up? Perhaps ask support staff to turn on the machines well before the workshop. Do the computers require login details? If so, obtain these and prepare cards to place by each computer (or if everyone shares the same details you can simply write these on the whiteboard).

▶ Check the internet connection speed (you can use a free service like speedtest.net). What happens if you log in to multiple computers? Does the speed drop significantly? Even if you cannot access the room where you will teach, you can get an idea of the local network speed by trying computers in a different room.

▶ Check how overhead projectors and other equipment work. Are they near power points? If not, can they be moved easily, or will you need extension cables? Do remote controls and other portable devices have batteries and are there replacements?

▶ Check out microphones and speakers, if you use them. Is the sound clear? How do you adjust the volume?

Check out your participants

If you plan to ask participants to use computers or other technology during the workshop, it is important to enquire with your sponsor or find out in other ways whether they have the necessary skills. One of your authors vividly remembers giving a workshop on computer-assisted language learning, when one of the participants picked up the mouse and moved it across the computer screen. A valuable lesson was learned that day.

It is not always possible to check participants' knowledge beforehand and one alternative is to start off with a simple task on the computer (perhaps as they come in at the start of the workshop), such as going to a website and logging in. Have this instruction up beforehand on the screen. You will quickly be able to identify those who may need more attention. If possible, seat people together who can help each other.

Be ready to abandon the technology

Prepare every workshop on the assumption that the technology will fail. Table 3.3 lists some common problems and ways of dealing with them.

▶ Using a microphone

Most workshops are conducted with small groups and there is normally no need to use a microphone. However, sometimes you may be asked to run a workshop for a large number of participants, or you may choose to use a microphone if you do not wish to strain your voice, especially when attempting to draw participants' attention when they are busy working in groups. You may also need to pass a microphone to someone in the workshop who wants to speak but has a very quiet voice.

There are four types of microphones:

(a) The fixed microphone, usually attached to a lectern. This style of microphone is not particularly helpful for workshops, as you will need to return to the lectern every time you use it. When the organisers ask you about your equipment needs beforehand, suggest that you don't want this type. Not all organisers have the idea that a workshop is not a talk.

(b) The wired microphone. This usually sits in a stand but can be removed. It offers some room for you to move around, but only for as far as the cable reaches. It can be cumbersome to avoid getting the cable wrapped around participants' chairs and desks and so on. Again, if there's a choice, avoid this one.

(c) The wireless microphone. This type of microphone gives you more flexibility. Its downside is that you need to hold it in your hand, limiting your movement. Its advantage is that you can hand it to a participant.

(d) The lapel microphone. This is the ideal type of microphone for work-shops. It clips onto your clothes and allows you to walk around and use it without the need to hold it. The only disadvantage of Type (c) is that it's more tricky passing it around to other speakers in the group.

Speaking into a microphone can take some getting used to. Here are some general hints.

▶ Always practise with a colleague or friend beforehand, to check the volume and sound quality. Ask the other person to stand at the front of the room and speak in a normal voice. Walk around the room to see how well you can hear everything. Is the volume right? Is the sound pleasant (for example, not too 'tinny' or distorted)?

▶ Now ask your colleague to walk around the room. Microphone types (c) and (d) work with a receiver – the further you move from it, the worse the sound quality will be. Finally, ask your friend to let you know how your own voice sounds as you do these different moves. Not everyone speaks at the same volume.

▶ Some receivers are more powerful than others, so it pays to find out what your maximum range is. If possible, you could move the receiver to a different location.

▶ Many speakers who are new to using microphones speak too loudly. As a rule of thumb, imagine you are talking without a microphone to the people sitting in the front row.

▶ Keep your normal speaking style. Some people's voices become flat when speaking into a microphone.

▶ When using a lapel microphone, make sure to place it somewhere you will not accidentally touch it, or cover it. Do not put it on your jacket if you intend to take it off later.

▶ Also, be careful not to place it too close to your mouth (it may pick up breathing sounds), or too far away (it may not pick up everything). Trial and error before the workshop is the key.

▶ Be aware that sometimes microphones can produce 'feedback' (a loud, high-pitched noise). This can happen when the microphone is near to a computer's speaker, for example. Simply move the microphone a bit further away.

YOUR TURN

What are some of the distracting uses of a microphone you have expe-rienced? How could these have been resolved?

Space issues

▶ **What is the optimal environment for a workshop?**

QUESTION

'I have noticed as a participant that I learn much better in some environments than others. How do I create a space that is most conducive to learning?'

Although we do not always have the luxury of choice, ideally workshops are held in spaces that have the following qualities:

▶ Well-ventilated and not too hot. Stuffy air will quickly tire the most enthusiastic of participants. If ventilation is not sufficient, open windows and a door to create an airflow. Ventilators, although noisy, can be helpful in hot situations. Slightly cooler is better than too warm.

▶ Bright. Where insufficient daylight is available (or the sun is too strong), good lighting is essential and has been shown to directly affect participants' concentration levels.

▶ Spacious. Unlike in regular classrooms, in workshops participants are likely to walk around a lot, to sit in groups and to work on posters or with other materials. Insufficient space will have a direct impact on the success of the workshop. Don't forget that you will also need additional space for yourself, to be able to easily move from one group to the next.

▶ Ideally, you have access to breakout rooms so that different groups can work independently.

▶ Flexible. Ideally the furniture needs to be movable. This is the most common problem with spaces for workshops where desks are fixed in long rows. Ideally, desks should be light and easily moved and put together with other desks to create new configurations.

▶ Large workspace. Individual desks should be able to be put together to create a larger workspace, or alternatively, large tables could be set up around the room.

▶ Sound-proof. Workshops are noisy environments. Unless the adjacent rooms are not occupied, the room needs to be somewhat soundproof so as not to disrupt others. Carpets in the room also help keep the noise levels down for participants themselves when discussions are in full swing.

- Wall space. For hanging up posters, for example.
- Adequate equipment, properly installed. If you will be using an overhead projector, for example, it needs to be set up so that there are no cables lying on the floor that someone could trip over, that the screen is easy to raise and lower, and that it is visible from all around the room.
- Nearby facilities. Ideally toilets are located nearby, as are facilities for breaks. A park or some other place for participants to take a break is ideal.
- Creative tools, such as games and instruments, are sometimes advocated and can be surprisingly effective, even with most 'serious' people!

Although beyond most facilitators' control, the design of the room also has an impact on learning (de Korte, Kuijt and van der Kleij, 2011). Putting up some posters or displaying sample materials can make a difference.

Again, although this is not a must, we recommend making sure there is water set up for everyone in the group (even if there are tea breaks scheduled). Dehydration is the most common cause of loss of concentration. In addition, having some lozenges in a bowl can be very helpful.

▶ Inadequate facilities

On arrival, presenters sometimes find themselves in rooms that are unsuitable in one or more ways. The unfair aspect of this is that attenders often think it is the fault of the person who has arrived from elsewhere to lead the event, when of course it's an on-the-spot organisational problem. Here is some advice based on experience in many countries.

1 Aim to arrive at the location early, so that problems and solutions can be discussed before the participants arrive.
2 Never rely completely on one means of communication. Powerpoint, to state the obvious, relies on having a proper supply of electricity, not to mention a data projector and large screen.
3 Tactfully invite the organiser to apologise to participants for any fault that is his or her responsibility. The organiser can always be invited to blame a third (absent) party!
4 If the room is very crowded, announce that there will be five-minute breaks (or longer) every so often.

▶ **Inadequate seating**

QUESTION

'The other day I arrived in this horrible little room, with fixed desks in rows. I was glad to get out after the three-hour workshop. I think the participants were too. What else could I have done but make the most of it?'

Although far from ideal, the above scenario is unfortunately rather common. Here are some possible remedies:

By coming early, you may be able to ask the organisers to find a better room.

If that is not possible, maybe you can use some common spaces, like hallways – for example, when breaking up into two groups, one group could work outside. By rotating the groups, at least everyone gets some fresh air.

Both of us have conducted workshops outside, sometimes out of necessity (in Yemen), or because the lawn outside the cramped classroom looked far more inviting. In situations where there are not too many distractions (e.g. traffic), this can work well.

Where the above are not possible, try to let people change places occasionally. Although that will not improve the difficulty of people working in small groups, at least it is not as static as remaining seated in the same place.

Get participants to work not only with their neighbours to their sides, but also with the people behind and in front of them.

Cultural issues

Workshop presenters who are working in a culture other than their own would expect to have to consider cultural issues when planning and conducting their sessions. However, many workshops in every country would today be likely to include people from a range of cultural backgrounds.

Identities

Each of us has multiple identities: our ethnic group, our part in a family, our work status and so on. When it comes to a collection of people at a workshop, their identities will overlap (and yet differ) in a number of ways.

The most visible identity that usually emerges when a group of people meet is ethnicity. Then once they start talking, the language identity becomes audible. As a broad guideline, if the examples given at the workshop (pictures, anecdotes, audiotapes) can reflect some of the differences within the group, then people are more ready to take ownership of the new ideas.

One warning would be not to make assumptions about participants' identities, particularly on the basis of appearance. An individual who might, at first glance, appear to be from one part of the world, could turn out to be the descendant of someone who migrated to another country several generations ago.

Language differences

By 'language differences' we don't mean whether people want the workshop to be conducted in English, German, Chinese or Hindi, to name just a few. We mean the language differences that can exist amongst the speakers of one language. Recently it was mentioned that half of the listeners looked blank when a speaker described something as 'setting the Thames on fire'. Although, to the speaker, this probably seemed like a simple metaphor, to many of the listeners it meant absolutely nothing. As well as those who had never heard this idiom before, there were those to whom the name 'The Thames' meant nothing.

When choosing illustrations, ask yourself what your normal source of illustration might be and then consider adding to your repertoire so that everyone has something to relate to. Here are some examples:

Sports metaphors
References to food
Historical illustrations
Geographical examples
Traits often associated with animals.

Then there is the issue of body language. This can affect interaction between the presenter and participants in various ways, as these questions about monitoring group work suggest.

'How close should the presenter stand to a group when approaching them?'

'Would it be acceptable for the presenter to put a hand on the shoulder of a participant, and would it make a difference whether they were the same or different genders?'

'Should the presenter stand over the group or draw up a chair to be at their level?'

Competition v. cooperation

One difference between people from different cultures can be the extent to which they prefer competitive or cooperative activities. Of course there are individual differences within one culture, too, on this question. A presenter could ask questions beforehand about this, so as to avoid setting tasks which rely too heavily on one or the other element.

Changing countries

Presenters in countries other than their own are most likely to have given thought to the topic of cultural issues. Some workshop presenters find themselves seen as 'outsiders' by the people they are working with. This feeling can come about because the presenter comes from a different professional or work area, or is seen as having more education but fewer practical skills, or, as in the case of the following vignette, is from a different country.

Look at an account from a Western teacher who has lived in China for many years.

VIGNETTE

The outsider

'One of the challenges of giving workshops comes when you are viewed as the outsider giving advice in a situation you don't completely understand. This challenge is exacerbated when giving workshops in a country that is not your own. In China where I live, I am literally referred to as an outsider (*waiguoren*), and this outsider status has been evident as I've given workshops to university and middle school teachers around my province. Their reluctance to trust me is understandable. I can never fully comprehend their situations. Moreover, even if I were to teach their classes, the participants would react to me differently. I'm a *waiguoren* in their eyes too.

At the university where I'm employed, I've recently been able to "get over the hump" with some of my colleagues. I do not have insider status, but I believe they no longer view me as an outsider. Relationship and length of relationship seem to come into play. With my colleagues, I'm the known entity who has taught at their university for 10 years and the teacher who taught many of them in their student days. For the last year, I've also been hosting English Corners with them that have become more a teacher support group than anything else. We've developed mutual respect and reciprocity. I ask their advice, and they ask mine. They listen to my ideas, and I listen to theirs. I attempt to rejoice in their successes and empathise with their failures, and they do the same for me. When I recently gave them the same workshop I've given to middle school teachers around the province, their reaction was different. To the middle school teachers, I may simply be the *waiguoren* who is offering an hour or two of entertainment while they take a break from the classroom. I fully expect my colleagues, however, to come back in a few weeks with stories of how they've applied my ideas. A good dose of reality (and humility) is on the way, though, when I give workshops later this semester in two new venues, and I return to my outsider status.'

M. K. Smith, China

Some situations, such as the one above, have no easy answers. The decision about who is the best person to run the workshop is usually made by the organiser. After that decision has been made, and the presenter has arrived at the site, occasionally it is a participant who feels the match between presenter and audience is not a good one.

Presenter issues

▶ **Stage fright**

Stage fright affects the majority of workshop presenters at some point. The impostor syndrome (Clance, 1985) is the well-documented phenomenon whereby even highly experienced professionals feel they are somehow cheating the audience, that they know less than they actually do, and fear being 'found out'. On the one hand, workshops are more intimidating than, for example, lectures, in the sense that you are working more closely with people and there is less opportunity to shut yourself off or create distance from the participants. On the other hand, this also makes workshops potentially a more participatory and friendly environment. Everyone has the chance to contribute and there is less time for participants to scrutinise the presenter. Also, some presenters actually consider they have a more natural role as they communicate with small groups and individuals in a way they can't when standing at the front. How do organisers deal with stage fright?

Many books have dealt with this challenge for presenters (we mention a couple at the end of this section).

Combatting stage fright in workshops

The first, reassuring, point to recognise is that workshops give many more opportunities for presenters to overcome their fears. Specifically, workshops allow you to:

Talk to the participants

One of the major advantages of workshops is that the number of participants is usually small. Both of us make it a habit to wait by the door or in the room and to say a few words to as many of the participants as possible as they come in. The participants enjoy the personal welcome and it gives us a chance to connect with them and find out a few things about them. This makes the whole experience a lot less daunting. This, of course, means arriving even earlier, so that people don't have their first view of you as you bend over the equipment.

Minimise the distance between you and the participants

One good point about workshops is that you can (literally) remove the 'stage' from stage fright. Most workshop participants will not be surprised, and in fact may expect you to walk around the room, join groups, sit down, and so on. During the pre-session check of the environment, make sure there are extra chairs for you to use. This means that there is a lot less physical distance between you and the audience, as with large classes or lectures, where presenters frequently report feeling scrutinised.

Get to know the participants better

Another advantage is that most workshops last longer than classes or lectures, giving you more time to relax and to hear from participants. One way to do this is to use an ice-breaker activity or even to start with a simple activity that requires every participant to share a reflection or experience. This usually quickly dissolves the 'wait and see' attitude adopted by some participants.

As the workshop progresses, making an effort to talk to people as much as possible; asking about their opinions and work contexts will help to create an inclusive and mutual relationship that is very difficult to achieve in other types of teaching.

Coffee breaks are another chance for you to meet and mix. This is another reason for being early. Then at break time you have a minimum of preparation tasks.

Get the participants to do the talking

Related to the above, let participants do some of the talking, especially if you know that you need some time yourself to settle into the workshop.

General advice

The suggestions below probably apply to all teaching and professional situations that involve a degree of anxiety.

Be rested

Fretting about a workshop the day and night before is not helpful. A good night's sleep has been shown to make all the difference. Do not rush before the workshop. Make sure everything is set up the day before or, if that is not possible, arrive early enough to complete all preparation and still have time for a quiet moment.

Breathe well

Many of us take very shallow breaths, even more so when we are busy or anxious. Basic breathing exercises can greatly help in calming our nerves.

Drink enough fluids, but not stimulants

Dehydration is common among presenters, as they are nervous, perspire more, talk a lot and in other ways dehydrate more quickly, and at the same time they often forget to drink during the longer workshops. Another common problem is that the tea and coffee offered during breaks are not the best drinks to rehydrate. Water is best. And minimise or avoid alcohol the night before. To avoid a dry mouth, a lozenge or peppermint can be quite helpful (but not gum).

Plan your transport

One of us recently had the experience of needing to catch an aeroplane, train and then taxi to the location. Plenty could have gone wrong with the timing. Better to be filling in time at some nearby café then to be running in late.

A friendly face

If you are very concerned, ask a colleague or friend to be in the audience. This can be very reassuring.

Related advice is to have a 'safe face' to turn to in the audience. Perhaps there is someone who looks particularly friendly or who is very enthusiastic. If you do feel anxious, briefly focusing on that person can be a help.

Practice makes perfect

Although it is true that for some presenters, stage fright is a lifetime challenge, for most others, initial anxiety disappears after a few workshops. If the first time was difficult, do not expect the next time to be equally challenging.

Take classes

Public speaking classes, including Toastmaster classes, are one way to get practice in a safe environment.

YOUR TURN

Do you suffer from stage fright in teaching? How do you deal with this? Now ask three colleagues the same questions.

▶ Not enough preparation time

QUESTION

'Yes, it's my own fault but the workshop is in a few days and I don't know if I'm going to have enough time to do a good job with it. Any shortcuts?'

If not a shortcut, it is good to know that some activities are remarkably versatile. Most experienced workshop facilitators have a repertoire of activities that they adapt for different topics and purposes. This could be a debate, with different 'teams' getting different kinds of information; a different workshop topic would simply require different information, or it could be a 'judge and jury' type activity where two teams have to create and present a series of arguments. Where such activities can be adapted, you will have a reasonable idea of the practical demands (e.g. technology, handouts) and the amount of time the activity takes.

Another option is to draw more on others' work than you normally would. With the proper acknowledgement it is entirely feasible to use content, activities and even materials (e.g. Powerpoints) from other presenters. Obviously you would not want this to form the bulk of your workshop content, but if you are short of one or two parts of your workshop, this can be an option and can in fact bring in a 'fresh' additional voice.

Although not good pedagogical practice, at times it may be necessary to look at activities that take up more time, simply in order to fill out a programme. Certain kinds of activities, such as projects (see p. 115), involve pre-teaching, a great deal of preparation work, considerable time for their execution, and often a presentation element where participants report back to each other.

▶ Last-minute substituting for a sick colleague

QUESTION

'The other day I got a panicked call late at night from a colleague asking if I could please take over her workshop the next morning as she was coming down with a cold. Naively, I agreed. The workshop was a disaster. Should I have said no?'

This is one of the hardest decisions as workshops, of course, involve a lot more than simply reading out someone's notes. Even if you are quite familiar with the subject, it is the activities that make workshops come alive. Here are some general tips to deal with this situation:

▶ A very obvious point, but do make sure to get *all* the materials from your colleague. Not just handouts, Powerpoints and notes, but also seemingly trivial things like a schedule with estimated start and end points for the different parts of the workshop, and practical notes such as information on where the toilets are. As this is a last-minute substitution, you will not have much time to think about these aspects yourself.

▶ Focus on the activities more than the content. What is it that participants are expected to *do*? How will you handle the activities?

▶ Read up on the different activity types (see p. 68) and the different types of learning they support. Make sure you understand the intended learning outcomes of the different activities. If you don't, your audience almost certainly won't.

▶ Don't be afraid to substitute or delete content or tasks you are not comfortable with. Workshops are very personal in that facilitators choose examples, and activities, that they are most familiar with. Make sure to add your own.

▶ Personalise the workshop by including your own experiences and anecdotes. Depending on how much time you have to prepare, see if you have some materials (documents, videos, websites) you have used in the past or have created yourself.

▶ Ask your colleague if there are additional materials that were not included in the final version of the workshop resources; some of these you may be more familiar or comfortable with.

Be honest with attenders. Let them know that you were asked to do this last night and that you were delighted because it's a topic you feel enthusiastic about. However, if they notice any timing problems, that will be the reason.

▶ First time facilitating

QUESTION

'Okay, so I've read this book, and I think I've taken all the advice on board ... My first workshop is next week. Getting nervous! Any last-minute advice?'

The key is to take it easy on yourself. As with all new skills, this one will take practice. Expect some things to go wrong, and see them as an opportunity to learn. Rather than worry about things not going to plan, perhaps make a quick (mental) note to review a particular point later. Do not get disheartened. As most experienced facilitators will tell you, workshops seldom go entirely to plan. The flexibility to adapt to a change in circumstances (more or fewer participants than expected, an activity not working out as you expected) comes with practice.

For a first workshop we recommend creating more content than you think you will need, so as to be able to choose a different activity if necessary. (Of course, do not force yourself to cover everything you created!) If you have time, it is also useful to do a trial run, if not of the entire workshop, then at least of one or two activities. This will give you a sense of how long activities take, anything in the instructions that might be unclear and the kinds of questions participants come up with. You could do this with just three or four willing colleagues, for example, so as to mimic one workshop group.

A good strategy is to set yourself up for success by starting off with content or an activity you are very familiar with and that you can expect to go well. That way you will feel more confident with the rest of the workshop.

A final word of advice is to give yourself plenty of time for the workshop; do not schedule anything too strenuous before the workshop and leave enough time to prepare, double-check the technology, and so on. Do take care of yourself; keep up your fluids and try to get a good night's sleep.

▶ Choosing a delivery style

Plenty has been written about the range of learning preferences and styles, but less is written about teaching styles. Petty (2004) uses the term 'the teacher's toolkit' to describe all the ways there are of teaching.

A starting point to identifying your skills could be to check this list of teaching skills. Give yourself an A for the skills you feel confident about, B for those you can do moderately well, and C for those where you feel weak.

→ Holding the attention of a group when I talk to them   A   B   C
→ Explaining difficult ideas clearly   A   B   C
→ Demonstrating practical skills   A   B   C
→ Giving helpful feedback to others who try out   A   B   C
   practical skills
→ Asking questions that call on various levels of thinking   A   B   C

→ Writing interesting case studies   A   B   C
→ Thinking up relevant role-plays   A   B   C
→ Encouraging participation by shyer people   A   B   C

Hopefully, you have more As than Bs and Cs. For those areas which you feel need developing, follow up some of the references in the index of this book.

Dealing with on-the-spot problems

One presenter reports on her experience running a workshop in which people from a range of professional backgrounds were attending to learn presentation skills. Here is what she noticed.

VIGNETTE

'Some of the people who were most communicative, humorous and interesting at morning tea and lunch breaks became wooden when they stood at the front to practise their presentations. I asked them why they hid their innate communication skills when they had to address the group. Here are two of their answers.
   "We thought that's how public speakers should talk."
   "My normal talk is too informal. I need to sound more professional when I'm talking to an audience."'

It is true that once upon a time, public speaking meant using a special voice and pitch sometimes associated with elocution lessons. If you listen to recordings of radio broadcasts from fifty years ago you realise how different the expectations have become over the years. Here are some more specific suggestions.

Using your voice

Today the fashion is to be oneself, at least within limits. Limits include making sure that everyone can follow clearly what you are saying and that your voice is interesting enough to keep them awake. Here are some ways you can do this.

CHECK YOUR VOLUME
Most of us don't know how we sound to an audience. We may be falling into any of the following traps.

1 Overstraining our voices when we are already perfectly audible.
2 Failing to make use of the sound system available.
3 Speaking mainly to the front half of the room.

There are one or two ways around these problems, starting with the idea of getting feedback from a friend. You need to go into a large room, ask the friend to sit right at the back, and then start speaking. Putting a recording device at the back and checking yourself is second best.

CHECK THE SPEED OF YOUR DELIVERY

Although a workshop is not just about listening to the presenter, there will be times when you need to speak to everyone. Having variety in your voice is one way to keep a roomful of listeners awake. Variety can come in various ways.

One kind of variety relates to speed of delivery. You may be a particularly fast or slow speaker or your regular delivery may be at an average speed. If you're not sure how to describe your conversational speaking speed, ask someone.

Whatever your usual speaking speed, when you are addressing a number of people, try changing for different effects. To make a particularly important point, slow down. That can include pauses ... but ... not ... between ... words. Try pausing at the end of a sentence or occasionally mid-sentence. Sometimes saying the same thing twice helps, but signal that this is what you are doing.

'Let me say that again.'

Practise varying your speed by timing yourself beforehand as you say the same paragraph at two, or even three different speeds.

VARY YOUR INTONATION

As we speak, our voice rises and falls, usually to emphasise a point or ask a question. At other times the voice rises because of a fashion. For instance, in some parts of the English-speaking world teenage girls have been noticed to raise their voice at the end of each sentence even when it's not a question.

Next time you listen to a speaker, start to notice the way the voice rises and falls. Advertisements on radio and television are often a good example of extremes in intonation in order to make a point. Then try recording your own voice saying the same thing two or three times with different intonation.

WATCH FOR ANNOYING TRAITS

At the risk of putting people off ever standing in front of an audience, let's list some of the little idiosyncrasies that people report in end-of-workshop evaluation forms. Watch out for them!

Clicking a ballpoint pen while talking
Constantly clearing the throat
Giving nervous little coughs or laughs
Repeating the same 'fillers': *um, OK, right* ...
Waving the prompt notes around
Overuse of certain phrases ('in this regard ...', 'to an extent', etc.)
Sipping water too often
Adjusting hair or clothes.

WATCH YOUR STANCE

People give different advice about a speaker's stance. Some say, 'Don't move. It only distracts people.' Others say, 'Keep moving. You want to look as if you are interacting with the attenders, not delivering a monologue.' Most advice from professionals favours moving.

Like much of the other advice, the best suggestion probably lies somewhere between the extremes. Don't be afraid of moving from the front of the room. If everyone is to be watching the front, as, for instance, when watching a Powerpoint presentation, the speaker can occasionally move to the back of the room and speak from there. This has several advantages:

▶ People at the back have the chance to hear better than those at the front.
▶ People are likely to concentrate more, as a change in the environment means cognitive engagement is kept up.
▶ Attention is taken away from the presenter in favour of the workshop content.
▶ The presenter has a chance to see what the visuals look like at a distance.

Here are some other suggestions that we and colleagues have found work well:

Tell anecdotes
Distribute handouts
Use trainees' names
Use visual aids
Ask questions

Personalise your presentation
Use humour (but be careful with this)
Use nonverbal communication
Mix up your techniques
Use a team-teaching approach
Use music
Take breaks
Show enthusiasm.

Use team teaching

The idea of having more than one teacher in a classroom at the same time is not new, particularly in classes of young children, but what might a 'team' look like in a workshop?

A 'team' can be as small as two people. In fact that is the most common use of team teaching. It can also be three or more people, but the bigger the team, the greater the need for one person to volunteer to be the overall organiser. A team can operate with both (or all) members in the room at the same time, moving round during group tasks. Here, based on a mixture of theory and examples, are considerations for people considering team teaching roles in a workshop.

ADVANTAGES OF TEAM TEACHING: A BURDEN SHARED

The first advantage that comes to many people's minds when they are offered the chance to team-teach is that the work is halved. In the best scenario, that is the case, although some report that they spend more time planning when they have to do it jointly than they do for solo planning. Also, as we see in examples below, the arrangement doesn't always mean that the person not presenting something can wander off for a coffee.

RANGE OF INPUT

The usual reason for sharing the role of presenter is that amongst two or more people each one has a specialty. Workshop attenders can hear from a number of 'experts' throughout the time. The input could divide itself out like this:

Theory ... application
The big picture ... the details
Examples from different workplaces
The experienced presenter ... the less experienced presenter.

At other times the presenters' skills are very similar. In the following vignette there is one example of team teaching which was used to model a process.

VIGNETTE

'Our topic is about customer relationships. You can give general guidelines but there will always be some new situation that people will report. We use role-play quite often between the three of us. One or two will be the customer and the other the service provider. We try to bring in some humour by exaggerating slightly, then we'll suddenly stop the role-play and invite people say what they'd do next.

Sometimes they'll tell us and we'll try to put their idea into practice. Other times we'll invite people to work in pairs, sort out a solution and present it to the group.'

DOWNSIDES OF TEAM TEACHING: EQUAL OR COMPLEMENTARY ROLES?
There can be pitfalls of team teaching, as this vignette shows.

VIGNETTE

'Two of us were asked to run a workshop for young adults preparing to apply for their first jobs. They were people who had left school with minimum qualifications and therefore, in many cases, low self-esteem.

We had been chosen as workshop leaders because we complemented each other in life-experiences and in our possible links with the attenders. We were about the same age, and one male, one female. I had been a school teacher while he had experience working in a factory. He was bilingual, one of his languages being that spoken by many of the participants. I was monolingual.

The workshop was to last a week. After the first session I was so concerned about how poorly we seemed to be going as a team that I asked a colleague to sit in the back and give me some feedback. Her analysis was quite simple, if humiliating for me. Apparently I was too patronising to my fellow-presenter. It seemed that, whereas I had thought we were sharing the up-front time, what was actually happening was that I came across as the leader. Worse than that, apparently I "invited" my colleague to take a turn at speaking, using a patronising tone of voice each time. The result was that the workshop participants saw the leader who most reflected their future roles as someone who had to be told when to speak.

There were more faults on my part but let's leave it at that! Only a good friend would have had the courage to tell me my faults.'

This anecdote illustrates one or two points about shared roles. The most obvious point is how difficult it can be to share in a genuinely equal way. Another is that goodwill is not enough. In this case the writer was humble enough to invite in someone whose advice she was willing to take.

A second pitfall in sharing the leadership role can be the planning process. Agreeing in plenty of time on answers to questions about options like the following, can help overcome these pitfalls.

1 Is the choice of sub-topics to be negotiated between the presenters or allotted to each according to their strengths?
2 Will the time slots be clearly defined as belonging to one person or another, or will there be flexibility as the workshop proceeds?
3 Who decides whether or not to respond to the attenders' requests such as 'Could we have more on that topic?'

The account in the following vignette shows how two people jointly planned and taught a workshop in a different country.

VIGNETTE

'Two of us from the same country were invited to travel to another country to present a seven-day workshop. Each of us had knowledge and experience in the same field, although we had found in the past that one of us preferred talking about the theoretical aspects of the topic while the other enjoyed giving practical applications. We knew from experience that we could work together on this basis.

A couple of months before the event, we met to map out the broad timetable, including the parts of the days for which each of us would be responsible. We then did our planning separately but emailed each other details of our sessions. We agreed that we could be flexible if it seemed that someone needed more time. (There didn't seem to be a problem with needing less time!).

We sat in each other's sessions, occasionally adding something by invitation or even spontaneously. This seemed to work well, especially when someone asked a question about what one presenter had said and the other presenter was able to clarify it in a different way.

We met at the end of each day to check on whether any adjustments needed to be made to the timetable for the following day.'

Use a range of styles

As we mentioned at the start of this section, just as there are many different learning styles, so there are many different teaching or presenting styles. Each style will help the audience in different ways. Check where you think you might stand on this list of pairs, and then note what different type of person you would enjoy co-presenting with at a workshop.

1 ☐ Enjoy telling a joke as a way of motivating people
  ☐ Prefer listening to and responding to other people's concerns than making up my own

2 ☐ Enjoy having everything mapped out in detail beforehand, including timing
  ☐ Prefer to be flexible on timing, responding to the mood of the attenders

3 ☐ Like to collect and present plenty of visuals
  ☐ Words are my strength

4 ☐ Like active interaction with participants
  ☐ Prefer show and tell

5 ☐ Enjoy going into detail
  ☐ Prefer the big picture

YOUR TURN

Together with a colleague, complete the Teaching Style survey (http://longleaf.net/teachingstyle.html). What are some of the differences in your approaches? How could you build on these?

Content issues

QUESTION

'Although so much information is available online, I actually find it surprisingly hard to find specific materials that are suitable for particular groups. How do others find good resources?'

▶ Finding good content

With workshops there is a clear interplay between *subject matter* (e.g. knowledge of guidelines for health workers on handling needles) and *activities* to test or practise that knowledge. You will therefore need to consider sources for both, including those that you will use for the workshop itself and those that you will give to your participants to engage with before and after the workshop.

You are probably quite familiar with sources for content in your subject area but sources for activities are harder to come by. Books such as this one are a good starting point but you should also try and share your experiences with other facilitators as much as possible to find out what has worked for them, in particular with specific groups. It always helps to have clear questions to ask, such as 'I see you have worked with these senior managers before. Were they comfortable using X technology or was this new to them?'

Another source of ideas is other people's workshops. At conferences, try attending workshops outside your normal field. See if you can identify:

▶ How new knowledge is introduced
▶ What types of practice are included
▶ What forms of grouping (individual, pairs, groups) are used
▶ What feedback is given
▶ What you liked and did not like.

Using existing content raises copyright and related issues, which we will turn to next.

▶ **Copyright and privacy issues**

QUESTION

'I have to admit that I've never given much thought to copyright. I usually cut and paste things from the internet and various articles and documents I have on my computer. But I'm wondering what the rules are – what can I use and what can't I?'

Some groundrules for a tricky area

Copyright laws are complicated and differ from one country to the next. For this reason it always pays to check with your organisation as to whether they have any guidelines. Of course, when delivering a workshop in another company or school, or even another country, this may not be practically feasible. Below are some general rules which will apply in most situations.

Always acknowledge your sources

This may seem obvious but it is often forgotten when the source is not a published book or article, but, for example, an artwork, a presentation you attended in the past, or advice from a colleague. If the idea is not your own, acknowledge it.

The other difficulty is with materials for which you have no source. Perhaps you jotted down some notes at a conference once, or have a collection of quotes without a source on your computer. A particular trap seems to be pages photocopied from a third source which, in turn, has not acknowledged its author. Try to find the source online and, if you can't, try to find an alternative. If you must use the original source, make it clear that you attempted to find the source but couldn't.

Apply 'fair use' in distributing materials

The UK copyright act of 1988 has a 'fair dealing' provision which allows copying of a reasonable proportion of a work for 'non-commercial research or private study'. The problem is that no clear definitions exist of what this means (and, of course, it is only one country's act), although often it is considered to be limited to making one copy of one article form one journal, or up to 5% of a book, but not multiple copies for classroom or electronic distribution, for example. In other words, you can use such materials to prepare for the workshop, but not hand them out. Interestingly, we have found that even commercial places where you pay for your photocopying will, rightly, stop short of copying more than a certain percentage from a book.

When in doubt, seek permission

Be on the safe side. If you are not sure if an image is 'Creative Commons' (see below), if an article can be copied, or a video shown, then be sure to contact the owner, the photographer, or the website host. Sometimes this can be done by your organisation, which can keep a record of sources for which permission has been given. This will also help other presenters.

Find materials that are copyright-free

Some materials are in the 'public domain'. This means that they are not restricted by copyright. Examples are books or music that were created more than 70 years (in most countries) after the death of their creator, such as the music of Mozart.

In addition, many authors, artists and other content creators make their works available under a Creative Commons licence. There are six different types of licence, each of which allows certain types of use. For example, the most open type of licence offered is called 'Attribution' or 'CC BY'. This allows users to distribute, remix, tweak, and build upon a work, even commercially, as long as the original creator is credited.

For workshop developers, articles, images, and other content that is provided under a Creative Commons licence are a particularly useful source.

Do not re-use participants' work without permission

If participants create a product during your workshop, you cannot use that product elsewhere without their permission. For example, during one of the activities they may produce a questionnaire. If you wish to use this question-naire yourself at a later date, you will need to both get permission and acknowledge them as the source. Have a permission form prepared ahead of time.

Your own copyright

Although uncommon, it is possible for an institution to ask you to sign an agreement that gives them the right to use any materials you have created for the workshop at future dates. You may or may not want this, so be care-ful. An even more restrictive agreement would stipulate that the materials you created for that workshop may not be used elsewhere. You need to be prepared for all these scenarios, including the most recent one asking you to send them your notes electronically. Of course, at this point you have no idea how they might be used, but be ready for the request.

Workshops and privacy

As with copyright laws, most countries have their own legislation regarding privacy. This includes regulations relating to what kind of information can be stored about participants and for how long, and if, and with whom, it can be shared. As with copyrights, it is best to be on the safe side. Never share personal data about participants without their explicit consent; even a seemingly innocuous blog post about a workshop that mentions what a paritcular person said or did can be out of bounds. It would be better not to refer to individuals (unless you have cleared this with them beforehand).

Similarly, be careful about how you store participants' contact details, grades (if any), and other personal information. As the facilitator you are responsible for keeping this data safe. For this reason it is good practice to only store what you really need, and only for as long as you need it.

Related to the topic of privacy is the use of participants' contact information in order to connect with them after the workshop. This could be for the purpose of sharing materials you mentioned during the event, or it could be to promote a future workshop. There is a fine line between being helpful and being considered invasive. For this reason we suggest leaving your contact details with the participants (on a handout or on the Powerpoint presentation), and inviting them to contact you if they want to keep in touch.

If you do decide to contact previous participants, always include an 'opt-out' option, such as a link that recipients can click to unsubscribe from future messages.

The Creative Commons website has a wealth of information about different types of licences and what they allow content to be used for.

You can find the Creative Commons website here: http://creative commons.org/

▶ **Mismatch between participants' levels, goals and actual needs**

> ## QUESTION
>
> 'My nightmare scenario came true the other day; I had spent ages preparing a workshop for a group of nurses who, I was told, needed to learn how to "handle difficult conversations with patients". It turned out that a few weeks earlier a nurse had been badly attacked by an angry patient and they were expecting to be taught how to defend themselves. I made the most of it, but it was not my finest hour. How could I have avoided this?'

Unfortunately, situations like the above do happen. Sometimes people's actual needs are misinterpreted as plans pass through the organisation's chain of managers and workshop organisers. Sometimes there may be other, political, reasons not to label workshops by the topic they are supposed to cover. The reality is that it is difficult to avoid some, occasional mismatch.

Of course, the best way to avoid this is to confirm the workshop content beforehand and ask questions about the participants and their:

Previous experience
Previous workshops/training they have taken
Needs and how these were established.

Ask to see any documentation that may be available, such as questionnaire results, reports, and so on. For longer workshops it may be helpful to email or talk on the phone to one or two participants. Another method is to send out an email asking participants to note down their expectations/hopes for the workshop. Check this with the organiser first though.

If the above information is not available, try to learn more about the participants by looking at their context, such as the organisation, sector, or region/country they work in. Websites of local professional organisations are often a good starting point. By looking at their recent reports, conferences and meetings you can get a feel for the current themes and concerns.

However, despite your best efforts, you may still find that the participants are expecting something different from what you have planned for them. It is better to find this out sooner rather than later, and it is better for this to happen in a constructive environment. For this reason most presenters take time early on to go over the workshop's goals and programme and invite comments. In addition, you can ask participants to prioritise the topics. By preparing two or three topics too many, you can leave out those that participants do not want to spend time on. Also ask participants whether they feel additional topics should be covered. There are then several options:

▶ It is a topic you are knowledgeable about and that you feel you can integrate.
▶ The topic is (partly) related to another topic you have planned to cover. Explain how the two are connected and how what you intend to do during the workshop will address the participants' concerns. Often people use different terms or may not realise that their questions form part of a larger subject.
▶ The topic is not related to anything you intended to cover and you are not knowledgeable on the subject.
Despite this, it may be possible to create an activity around the subject. In the second part of this book, a range of different workshop activities is covered; some of these rely more heavily on the presenter's input than others. For example, a discussion task that requires participants to find three arguments for and three arguments against a plan, relies more on the participants' knowledge and experiences. Up to a point, presenters can 'bridge' some of their own content with additional topics by encouraging participants' input. If in doubt, however, the best policy is always to be open and honest. Admit that the topic is not your area of expertise but offer to facilitate an activity around it. You can turn this kind of situation to your advantage by asking participants to prepare a short presentation or an argument for you. In this way you are drawing on their strengths and experiences.

If the main issue is that the content of the workshop is too easy or too difficult, then it is possible to adjust the level by:

(1) Leaving out some particularly difficult (aspects of certain) topics.
(2) Changing the activities. In Part 2 of this book we looked at different levels of knowing (page 82). Try to substitute, for example, a descriptive for a reflective task.
(3) Focus more on providing information rather than critical tasks for participants to complete.

▶ **Too much or too little content**

QUESTION

'Workshops take our time and money. It's not satisfactory to come away thinking it's been fun and a chance to meet interesting people. I want something more than that to get my teeth into and to report back to others. Is that reasonable?'

Workshops are notoriously hard to plan, as so much depends on the participants and how their knowledge, experiences, enthusiasm and so on affect how long it takes them to complete the various activities. As described on page 67, it is always good to try to design your workshop modularly so that you can easily swap a longer for a shorter topic or activity, especially towards the end of the workshop. Both of us usually include one or two 'optional' activities. The 'core' content of the workshop will almost always be covered and, depending on the time available, there may be one or two extension activities.

Not having enough content is rare. It is not difficult to allocate a bit more time to an activity if you feel you have enough time available. Nonetheless, in situations where what you prepared does not match participants' expectations (see the preceding section), this can happen. One way to fill a programme is to ask participants to prepare a short presentation on the subject of the workshop. Although a useful activity, this can be quite time-consuming.

Dealing with organisers

QUESTION

'The topic I've been asked to address is really not my strength. I don't want to seem difficult but I would rather cover a different topic. How can I suggest this?'

It is important to realise that often the requested topic is not fixed, but merely a suggestion. More often than not, the organisers will not fully know all the different aspects of the field that could be covered. Feel free to offer additional or alternative topics, perhaps showing how these relate to or flow from the originally requested subject.

If your workshop has to fit in with the theme of a larger event (such as a conference or a training week), be open-minded about the possible connections with your area of expertise. Both of us have often found that what seemed vastly different fields had numerous points of connection. Also, don't underestimate the benefits of offering an 'outside perspective'.

One thing that should be avoided, however, is not clarifying what will and won't be covered in your workshop. Always send in an outline, even if only in preliminary form, and get approval. This way there will be no misunderstandings.

In the unlikely event that you will be asked to cover a subject you really feel uncomfortable with (either because you feel you lack the expertise, or because it does not match your professional beliefs), do not hesitate to politely decline the workshop. One of us was once asked to conduct a workshop on a teaching method that the management wanted to promote, but for which there was no support in the university. In this case, a diplomatic response was needed. In the long term, it is better for your reputation not to take on workshops that put you too far out of your comfort zone.

▶ **Negotiating the length of the workshop**

QUESTION

'I've had both situations where the hosts wanted me to offer a workshop that was far too short for the subject, and cases where the opposite was true. How can I handle situations like this?'

It is important to clarify expectations in as detailed a way as possible. If a request for a workshop of a certain duration seems unreasonable, bear in mind that in many cases the hosts do not have anything like the same depth of knowledge about the topic as you do. Often also, organisers do not have as much time to spend thinking about what would be a suitable length of time for your specific subject. In other words, requests are often merely suggestions, not set in stone. Most organisers are grateful for a friendly counter-suggestion. In such cases it is best to submit a preliminary outline of the workshop, with the topics to be covered and estimated times for each. In this way you can let the organisers see your reason for needing more or less time. Also, make sure to highlight which sections could be left out in order to fit into the originally offered time slot. On more than one occasion we have experienced organisers realising that the topics were too important to be dropped, and more time was found.

However, there are situations where organisers are simply trying to fill out a programme, for example when there is a three-hour gap after lunch and before the afternoon plenary. In such cases there may be little room for movement. However, do consider the following options:

By having a look at the rest of the programme, you may find that it is possible to swap one event for another, so as to have more (or less) time.

If the slot is too long, perhaps you could consider doing two workshops instead of one, either on the same topic (so that more people can attend) or on two different topics.

If the amount of time is much too short, perhaps you could offer to do a presentation instead of a workshop.

▶ **Negotiating remuneration**

QUESTION

'I am a teacher, not a business person. I really have no idea how much to ask for. What is reasonable?'

For many educators this is a tricky topic. Few teaching qualifications prepare participants for this important aspect of their future careers, to the point where many educators will have never considered what their time and expertise are worth until they are asked by the host institution, 'What are your fees?' Especially for workshops, this is a difficult question to answer as the amount of preparation and travel time usually far exceed the duration of the workshop itself. And there is the matter of one's valuable knowledge and experience, which are more difficult to quantify. In addition, and at the risk of generalising, for many educators, simply the joy of teaching and their passion for the subject often come first. But this does not mean that financial matters are not important or that there should be an expectation to work for less, or indeed, for free.

'Early in my time of doing workshops I was nervous about stating a sum of money. After a few sessions when the "payment" turned out to be boxes of chocolate and local souvenirs I changed my tune.'

So, how does one determine a reasonable fee, and how should this, as well as other forms of compensation, be negotiated? A number of factors play a role in the fee you decide to set. These include:

Your field. It is a fact that workshop presenters in some fields are paid considerably more than in others. Business and investment workshops often charge considerable entrance fees to participants, and some of this goes to the presenter. It is not unheard of for highly regarded speakers to receive tens of thousands of dollars per session. Of course, this is not the norm and the key is to find out what other speakers *of similar stature* charge. For many people it is not easy to talk about money and it is best to raise the subject privately, and tactfully. Instead of asking for a specific fee, you could ask for a common *range*. Also, be specific about the type of teaching context (see below) you are asking about. Colleagues, current or former supervisors, and staff working in human resources may be good sources of information.

The host institution. A workshop given to a company is usually charged at commercial rates, whereas an event at a school or non-profit organisation may be charged at a lower rate. This does not mean that you should expect to work for free, as even non-profit organisations usually still have a budget for staff development and such.

Country. If you are invited to another country, it is important to take into account the fact that the purchasing power – or, what money is worth in that context – may be much higher or lower than in your home context. For example, the first time one of us was asked to give a workshop in Japan, the amount seemed staggeringly high, but in fact was the going rate. Likewise, both of us have given workshops in developing countries for free, or in exchange for accommodation and perhaps transportation to and from the venue (see below). It is not easy to determine what one should charge in another country and one way around this decision is to draw on external information. One of us uses the United Nation's Human Development Index (http://hdr.undp.org/en/statistics/) as an indication. The normal fee charged in the home context is 100%, and for other countries the fee will be raised or lowered proportionally.

One-off or return engagement? Of course, whether a workshop is a one-off event or a return engagement may have an impact on your fees. One of us regularly gives workshops at an institution in Singapore. The topic is usually the same and many of the materials and workshop content are similar. As a result, the amount of preparation time is much lower, and the fees can be lower too.

Negotiating fees

One of the most successful and least commonly used approaches is to simply ask what remuneration is available. Especially if you are new to giving workshops, or have not worked in a particular context before, you may not know what the going rate is for your type of work. By asking, you will usually get a reasonable reply, which will indicate what price range the institution is considering. If, for example, you were hoping to earn £600 for a session and the host institution offers you a free lunch but no fee, you know that the chances of reaching agreement will be slim. If, however, the institution offers £500, you could write back and explain why you think £600 would be reasonable (perhaps there is more travel time and cost involved than the organisation anticipated. Perhaps this is offered in addition to the fee, in which case the total is *more* than the £600 you had hoped for).

Quotations

Some institutions require you to submit a more or less formal quotation. You can download templates online that will make sure your quotation looks professional and includes all the necessary information, such as:

Your company name (or your own name if you do not have a company)
Contact details
Date and length of the event
Who the event is for (which department; also include the names of your contact person)
Number of hours' teaching time
Number of hours' preparation time
Travel time
Materials costs
Travel costs (e.g. tickets)
Per diem (see below)
Other costs, for example room and equipment hire, food and beverages, if not provided by the host institution
Your hourly rate (you can choose to use a different rate for travelling and teaching)
The total amount.

If you offer workshops frequently you could also look into web services that can automate the creation of quotations and invoices and keep track of payments, such as www.freshbooks.com and www.roninapp.com.

Additional compensation

There is a range of other forms of compensation possible. One that you will often see is the *per diem*. This is compensation, usually for costs associated with the event, such as food and beverage, and local transportation. Some institutions use the *per diem* as the fee for the event (sometimes this is done because some institutions are unable to hire and pay external staff, so in order to circumvent this, the *per diem* is inflated) and it can therefore seem very high. Be sure to confirm what the *per diem* is supposed to cover. Rather than asking for a higher free, sometimes it is easier to ask for a higher *per diem*. Be aware that, although '*per diem*' literally means 'per day', some institutions will give you a certain amount for the entire event, even if this is more than one day. One of the authors of this book learned this the hard way when a *per diem* of £120 for a four-day event turned out to be £30 per day.

Sometimes the *per diem* includes an allowance for you to make your own bookings for accommodation, but frequently this is compensated for separately, either by the institution making and paying for a booking for you, or by them setting a certain amount that you can then use to book accommodation, to be reimbursed later. It is important to always keep receipts, even if you are not expecting reimbursement, as this will help you go gauge costs better for future events, and also because host institutions sometimes ask for them.

Food and beverage are usually included in the *per diem*, but sometimes offered separately, usually included as part of a conference or events programme. In some expensive destinations this can be an important consideration. The first author of this book once found himself stranded in a luxury hotel where the event was being held, with the only available breakfast nearby being the £40 buffet in the lobby. This alone was more than the *per diem*.

Transportation can be a major cost, especially where it involves international travel. Some institutions make all the arrangements for you, including booking and paying for the travel. This can be convenient but it can also be inefficient – for example, if you have other travel plans before and after the event. You may be travelling from location A (your home) to B (the workshop location) then to location C (a conference), without wanting to return to A first. In this situation you could suggest to the institution that you obtain a travel quotation yourself for the *lowest suitable travel option* and then get permission to book that, for later reimbursement. On occasion, both of the authors of this book have written to our hosts to request that we travel with an alternative company, even though it was not the cheapest, for example because of much shorter travel times. Some institutions offer business class travel, but always check first, and usually it will be safe to assume that all travel will be economy class, at the lowest available fare. Do not forget to include local transportation. In some cities getting to and from the airport, for example, or to and from the event centre, can be a major cost.

Most of the above are actually forms of reimbursement, not compensation (as they simply cover the costs of conducting the event); however, other types of costs are a slightly different matter. For example, your hosts may organise sightseeing or other events for you. These can often be among the most pleasurable ways of getting to know another city or country, and are – if we are perfectly honest – certainly one reason why we enjoy workshops so much! Other benefits may be less tangible but could be important too. For example, we have seen many colleagues make mention of their own books or products, or even hand out flyers afterwards. The extent to which you promote other products or services is something you will need to consider carefully, however, and possibly discuss with your hosts. One thing that most likely will not raise any eyebrows is if you include your contact details in the handouts and make it clear you are available for other speaking engagements.

Invoicing

Unfortunately many large institutions have very complicated payment structures. One faculty may hire you to give a workshop in a particular department, which will be paid for out of a central fund, which will be processed by an external, outsourced accounts department. It is perhaps not surprising that sometimes invoices are not paid or take a long time to be cleared. The key is to have a system to track payments. The software mentioned above can help you do this. Also make sure to include all the relevant information. In addition to the information listed above under 'quotations', also include:

- ► Your bank account name and number
- ► Your bank address (especially in the case of international payments)
- ► Your business address
- ► A reference number or description for yourself, to enable you to identify the payment
- ► Your bank's IBAN or SWIFT (Europe) or routing (US) number
- ► Your GST/VAT number, if applicable

It is essential to keep copies of all receipts, so that when it comes to sending your invoice you have all the information handy. Programs like Evernote (www.evernote.com) make collecting these electronically easy.

► Declining invitations

Sometimes you are unable to accept an invitation to give a workshop. In Table 3.4 there are some common reasons for this, and some points to consider before writing back to your hosts.

If these suggestions do not work, it may be better to decline. Explain your reasons, but be political. Do not be afraid to turn down work if you think you will not be able to be successful, for whatever reason.

Table 3.4 Reasons for delining invitations

Reason	Response
You don't have time	Can the event be rescheduled? Can it be offered online?
Fees are too low	Is it possible to negotiate the fees, or perhaps the reimbursement for travel and other costs? See the section on 'Negotiating remuneration' (pp. 205–9).
You do not feel comfortable with the topic you have been asked to talk about	Are there any connections with your area of expertise? Some of the most successful workshops the authors of this book have given have been on topics not directly related to our fields, where the participants were enthusiastic to learn about concepts from another professional area. If you feel that is not possible, the best option is to write back to your hosts and explain what you *can* do (rather than emphasise what you cannot do). For example, you may be asked to give a workshop on dealing with harassment in the workplace and instead offer to talk about communication strategies. In our experience, hosts are often quite happy to consider a range of topics, so it pays to offer a list of alternatives.
You do not think the workshop or the event is useful/relevant	Sometimes presenters know that the reasons behind a host wanting to offer a workshop are either unclear or even disingenuous. A workshop on 'intercultural communication' could be just that, or it could be a prelude to staff being asked to work with an overseas team to whom part of their work is outsourced (the experience of one of the authors of this book). Sometimes experienced presenters can tell when what a company or institution wants is simply not feasible. It may then be safer, and better for your own reputation in the long term, to decline the invitation. One of us once wrote back with some suggestions for work the institution and its staff could complete first before we came to conduct a training event. A year later a letter arrived with a follow-up invitation and a personal note from the institute's director, with thanks for not offering the workshop prematurely.
The workshop is too long / too short / timed poorly	Offering a compulsory 8-hour workshop the day before the start of the holidays may not work. Although requests for workshops may sometimes be stated like fixed demands ('to give a four-hour workshop on 19 January with the following topics: ...'), these can usually be negotiated. Explain why you think the workshop deserves the timing and the time allocation it does.

▶ **Organising your own workshops**

QUESTION

'I have been considering running my own workshops as I usually end up doing all the work anyway. What should I think about?'

Organising your own workshops comes with its own challenges and rewards. You bear more risk, but also have greater control over the event, and of course, you get to keep the proceeds.

There are some specific considerations to take into account. Firstly, you will need to organise your own venue and this can be more challenging than you think. Whereas most companies and schools have suitable spaces for learning, the same cannot be said for many other buildings, where rooms may be noisy, stuffy, too small, with fixed furniture, and so on. Read the earlier sections on setting up the classroom (pp. 72–4), to help you identify suitable locations.

Another issue is insurance. Whereas most schools and companies have third-party and liability insurance, if you organise a workshop yourself you have to check with the room providers whether they are covered.

A further legal point to be aware of is that you will need to be extra careful to abide by any copyright regulations as you will be personally liable if you do not. Avoid the temptation of saving costs on photocopied materials and so on.

You will also need to do all the promotion yourself, and to take registrations and participants' details. Think about how you will store that information safely (you may want to read the section about technology on page 166).

One major advantage of organising your own workshops is that you will be able to retain any income yourself. However, you will, of course, also be liable for any costs, so do your calculations beforehand and include both all anticipated costs and an allowance for unforeseen expenses. The former could include:

Room hire
Catering (including your own)
Accommodation
Photocopying
Renting equipment

Transportation
Assistants, if any
Copyrights.

Unforeseen costs could be:

Renting a replacement laptop in case of breakdown
Costs for a taxi or a replacement ticket in case of delays
Participants who don't pay or do not show up.

Once you have considered all of these, decide if it will be financially viable to offer the workshop.

Also, be aware that organising workshops yourself makes you self-employed and this may affect the taxes you are liable for. We recommend that you speak with a tax advisor about this.

Promoting workshops

QUESTION

'It would be good if organisers didn't have a "one size fits all" advertisement for their workshops. I don't know how many times my staff come back and say, "You told us they'd ... and they didn't." Is it dishonesty or just carelessness?'

The amount and type of promotion you do for your workshop depends primarily on who organises it. If a company or school has invited you to give a workshop at their premises, it is likely that they will take care of advertising it. Especially if the workshop is intended for, or even limited to, employees of the organisation itself, there will be little scope or need for further promotion. That does not mean you cannot use the event to bolster your own CV or, for example, tweet about it, as long as you make it clear the workshop is not open to the wider public. In fact the safest way to do this when the event is closed entry is after the event. One point to be careful of is to check that the organisers, or the office responsible for promoting your workshop, are accurate in their description of the event. One of us has had several experiences with participants being promised unreasonable outcomes for the type and duration of the event, possibly in an effort to increase attendance.

The sequence of organising promotion often follows this pattern:

► They ask you if you would speak > you suggest a topic > they modify it and send it back to you.
► You return it in your own wording, asking to see the final copy before publicity happens > you hear nothing.
► You contact them again asking to see the wording > you change or approve it.
► Publicity happens.

If, on the other hand, the event is public, most organisations will greatly appreciate it if you help with promoting it, and if you are organising the event yourself this becomes crucial. Here are some common outlets:

Professional organisations – these often have websites or email newsletters that list events.

Mailing lists – the main concern here is to ensure your workshop content is relevant to the recipients, otherwise people will not appreciate your message. It is usually better to include the information in the email, and perhaps a link to further details online, than to attach particularly large files.

Personal website – especially if you frequently give talks, an up-to-date website is helpful, perhaps with a facility for people to book a workshop. There are many companies that will provide you with a customisable template-based site that includes this type of facility.

Social networking – increasingly important: a detailed discussion of this is beyond the scope of this book, but we do encourage you to subscribe to Twitter feeds, connect to Linkedin profiles, and follow authors and presenters on Facebook and Google+ and other relevant sites as much as possible to find out where and how they promote their talks.

Google ads and other online advertising sites let you create targeted ads that show up when people search for keywords. This can be a cheap way to reach potential participants.

YOUR TURN

How do you normally find out about interesting talks and workshops in your field? Do you mainly hear this from colleagues and friends, or read about it online? Find out where most of the information comes from, and this is where you will want to direct your efforts.

Promoting your workshop is about more than just naming a time and a place. It is important to be clear about the

Outcomes: what will participants learn? What will they be able to *do* after the workshop? Be very specific and comprehensive here.
Audience: who is it for?
Level/prerequisites
Date and time
Location
Price
Contact information: how do people contact you if they have questions? Where do they book?

Normally this organisational side will be handled by others. Most presenters don't want to be flooded with emails ranging from dietary requests to suggestions of different topics.

In addition, you can add:

Testimonials: these can be a very helpful way to share previous participants' experiences with prospective participants. There is no need to limit testimonials to individuals. After a successful workshop, ask your host institution or company to write one for you. Typically, the shorter and more succinct the better.

List of previous workshops and organisations: if you have given workshops at prestigious or well-known companies or universities, mention them.

A good workshop title is important, as most people do not take the time to read the full description of the workshop to decide if they are interested. Your title will need to raise interest and be descriptive enough to give participants an idea of what it is about (a subtitle can be helpful for this).

Evaluating workshops

QUESTION

'At almost every workshop I have attended or organised, there is the obligatory "feedback form". I have never quite understood the point of this. Where do the results go, and what is done with them?'

The move to answerability by speakers, teachers, presenters and others who speak as 'experts' has led to the development of various options for evaluating courses, and in our case workshops.

At the close of a workshop there is often an evaluation form to be filled in. Traditionally this is filled in by participants and lets the presenter know the answer to questions such as these:

'How well did the workshop measure up to your expectations?'

'What aspects were satisfying to you?'

'What could have been done differently?'

Answers tell the organisers (and the presenter) the impressions participants have at the end of the sessions. They don't tell them other aspects that could be useful for future sessions, such as:

'How do the sponsors feel about the session?'

'What are the long-term effects of the learning that took place?'

A number of issues are discussed in relation to these evaluation forms, including these:

What is the purpose of the evaluation process?
When should the evaluation be done?
Should a supervisor 'vet' them before the presenter sees them?
Should the feedback be anonymous?
Are the forms retained? For how long?

We now look at these questions one at a time.

The purpose of the evaluation

Here are some purposes for evaluating a workshop.

1 To guide organisers in their future choice of presenters and topics.
2 To guide presenters on future content and process.
3 Because the funders require it to be done.
4 For promotion purposes.

Naturally, each of these purposes determines the form of the feedback form.

Timing

The evaluation of learning done in a workshop parallels evaluation done in other areas of learning, except for one thing. The facilitator probably meets the participants once only, and therefore there is less time for this aspect:

(a) by the facilitator at the end of the session
(b) by the sponsor or organiser later.

Facilitator-led evaluation

The facilitator can decide where, on the spectrum of informal to formal, the evaluation is best done. Here are some methods that have worked.

▶ Self-reporting can happen informally towards the end of the workshop, when the participants are asked a question such as 'What is one point from today's session that you hope to implement later in your workplace?' This can be done in order, around the group, or people can be asked to raise their hands and mention something.

▶ A quick quiz provides participants with a chance to summarise their learning. As questions come up on the Powerpoint screen, they note a brief response. They then share their answers in twos or threes.

▶ Participants are given a moment to jot down a question that they would like clarified or to be given further information about. For this to work, there needs to be enough time left at the end. If the presenter's answers go over into what is seen as 'home time', attention will have wandered.

▶ Some presenters invite participants to share their experiences via email. This can be with the presenter only, or with others in the group. Many free websites allow you to set up a temporary group for participants to exchange ideas and questions.

Sponsor-led evaluation

The sponsor or organiser can evaluate learning in one or more of these ways.

▶ A traditional evaluation is completed immediately after the workshop, or sometime later.
▶ Focus groups can meet back at the workplace, and report on what they learned from the workshop.
▶ Organisers interview participants at a later date, one to one, to ask about their learning.
▶ If a certificate is to be awarded there may need to be a more formal test, perhaps a practical one if the workshop has been introducing new workplace practices. See the section on p. 122, about evaluating learning in workshops.

Sometimes the workshop evaluation shows that participants gained something from it that the facilitator hadn't intended, as the following vignette shows.

VIGNETTE

'The topics in my workshops involve family relationships and managing and understanding children's behaviour from a professional perspective. Although the focus is meant to be on training people to deal with situations when they arise, the case studies often provoke the sharing of stories about their own personal lives. That means we have to set high standards of confidentiality about what is reported later, by all present.

In the post-workshop evaluations, about 9/10 participants answer the question: "What did you enjoy most?" with statements like these: "telling my own story", "being with people who've had similar experiences".

It seems as if the outcomes stated by participants are not always the same as those intended by the organisers and presenters. Adult learners tend to process issues through the lens of their own experience, and while self-disclosure is not a goal of the workshop it seems inevitable that this would occur. As long as the facilitator is skilled to manage the process, it should not present a problem, and obviously the participants see it as a key learning process.'

Jill Worrall, New Zealand

Who sees the evaluation first?

The following report illustrates why it can be important not always to hand the evaluation sheets straight to the presenter.

VIGNETTE

'Once I worked in an organisation where the leader used to collect all the evaluation sheets and read them himself before showing them to the presenters. At first this seemed to me an invasion of privacy, but one case changed my mind. On this occasion he asked the advice of other senior staff, of whom I was one.

Here is why. It seemed that one attender had, anonymously, written a particularly cruel attack on a presenter. The writer wasn't to know the circumstances of the presenter's personal life at that moment but the leader did. He asked my opinion about withholding this particular form. Given the presenter's fragile state and the fact that almost all the other evaluations were positive, it seemed wise to withhold that one. Others might have felt differently, but to me the leader's action was compassionate.'

Of course there could be other circumstances where a presenter wanted to withhold one or more sheets. This can happen, for example, when evaluation feedback is used for promotion purposes. Like many other well intentioned ideas, evaluation sheets can raise ethical questions to which there are not always easy answers.

Should the feedback be anonymous?

There are, as so often happens, arguments for and against anonymous evaluations. The advantage of anonymous feedback is that people can speak frankly without fear of follow-up. On the downside, there is no answerability, particularly with vague negative comments, as people can't be contacted for clarification.

There is one other kind of feedback, which is given orally. Here, a small number of people are willing to sit informally with the organisers, and perhaps the presenter, to say what they learned from the workshop, highlighting its strengths as well as making suggestions for next time.

Are results retained?

The answer to this question depends on what the intended purpose is. If the idea is just to get some sort of statistical satisfaction survey, then once the results have been analysed and noted numerically there is no need to keep them.

Giving workshops to colleagues

QUESTION

'I recently went on a two-week course on financial reporting. When I came back my supervisor asked me to give a workshop to the rest of the accounting department. I feel very awkward. These are the people I work with every day and now suddenly I have to teach them. What will the think of me?'

Giving workshops to colleagues can be a daunting prospect for many, especially if some of the colleagues are your seniors or friends, but in actual fact the workshop format is ideal in this context. As workshops are more collaborative than, for example, a regular presentation, you can draw on everyone's experiences and strengths. Specifically:

▶ Start by inviting people's opinions and ideas on the subject.
▶ Identify questions that people have or areas that are unclear.
▶ Share ideas and suggestions, including your own.
▶ Guide the group towards a shared understanding and agreement.

Remember, you are there not to impose your view but to facilitate a structured discussion. If you prepare well and have all the relevant materials ready (e.g. documents, demonstrations, samples, follow-up reading) everyone will appreciate the opportunity to hear what you have to share. If you are particularly concerned about managers and other senior staff being present, emphasise the practical benefits of the workshops and highlight the key issues to be addressed and the intended outcomes. That way busy colleagues are more likely to contribute.

Emphasising everyone's role and the importance of their contributions should also extend to you; even if you have fewer years in the workplace than some of your co-workers, you do have experiences that others do not. This could be because of where you trained, a particular company or field you worked in before, or countries you have visited for your work. Look at your workshop not as a way of telling others how to do their jobs but as an opportunity to share your perspective; and to learn from that of others.

References

Arnold, J. (ed.) (1999). *Affect in Language Learning*. New York and Cambridge: Cambridge University Press.

Banas, Jennifer R. and Velez-Solic, Angela (2013). 'Designing Effective Online Instructor Training and Professional Development', in Keengwe, J. and Kyei-Blankson, L. (eds), *Virtual Mentoring for Teachers: Online Professional Development Practices*. Hershey, PA: Information Science Reference, pp. 1–25.

Biggs, John B. and Telfer, Ross (1987). *The Process of Learning*. Sydney: Prentice Hall.

Block, David (2003). *The Social Turn in Second Language Acquisition*. Edinburgh: Edinburgh University Press.

Block, David (2007). *Second Language Identities*. London: Continuum.

Brown, James D. and Rodgers, Theodore S. (2002). *Doing Second Language Research*. Oxford: Oxford University Press.

Burns, Anne (2010). 'Action Research', in Paltridge, Brian and Phakiti, Aek (eds), *Continuum Companion to Research Methods in Applied Linguistics*. London and New York: Continuum.

Carter, Ronald and Nunan, David (2001). *The Cambridge Guide to Teaching English to Speakers of Other Languages*. Cambridge: Cambridge University Press.

Clance, P. (1985). *The Impostor Phenomenon*. Atlanta, GA: Peachtree.

Cohen, Andrew D. and Macaro, Ernesto (2007). *Language Learner Strategies*. Oxford: Oxford University Press.

Crouch, C. H., Fagen, A. P., Callan, J. P. and Mazur, E. (2004). 'Classroom Demonstrations: Learning Tools or Entertainment?' *American Journal of Physics*, 72(6): 835–8.

Dean Brown, James and Rodgers, Theodore S. (2002). *Doing Second Language Research*. Oxford: Oxford University Press.

de Korte, E., Kuijt, L. and van der Kleij, R. (2011). 'Effects of Meeting Room Design on Team Performance in a Creative Task', Proceedings of the *Ergonomics and Health Aspects of Work with Computers* International Conference, Orlando, FL, 9–14 July 2011.

Dewey, John (1897). 'My Pedagogical Creed', *The School Journal*, LIV(3): 77–80.

Dörnyei, Z. (2001). *Teaching and Researching Motivation*. Harlow: Pearson Education.

Dosseville, Fabrice, Laborde, Sylvain and Scelles, Nicolas (2012). 'Music during Lectures: Will Students Learn Better? *Learning and Individual Differences*, 22(2): 258–62.

Farrell, Thomas S. C. (2007). *Reflective Language Teaching: From Research to Practice*. London: Continuum.

Freeman, Donald and Cornwell, Steve (eds) (1993). *New Ways in Teacher Education*. Alexandria, VA: TESOL (Teachers of English Speakers of Other Languages).

Gee, J. P. (2003). *What Video Games have to Teach Us about Learning and Literacy*. Basingstoke: Palgrave Macmillan.

Good, T. and Brophy, J. (1987). *Looking in Classrooms* (4th edn). New York: Harper & Row.

Hattie, John (2009). *Visible Learning: A Synthesis of Over 800 Meta-analyses Relating to Achievement*. London: Routledge.

Lamb, Terry and Reinders, Hayo (2008). *Learner and Teacher Autonomy*. Amsterdam: John Benjamins.

Lewis, Marilyn (1998). *Teaching English Language One to One*. Wellington: National Association of ESOL Home tutors, pp. 18–34, 'Setting Goals' and 'Measuring Progress'.

Lewis, Marilyn (2000). 'Frameworks for Feedback', *Guidelines*, 22(2): 5–8.

Lewis, Marilyn (2002a). *English Conversation Groups*. Sydney: New South Wales Adult Migrant Service [based on interviews in New Zealand].

Lewis, Marilyn (2002b). *Giving Feedback in Language Classes*. Singapore: RELC Portfolio Series.

McGrath, Ian (2002). *Materials Design and Evaluation for Language Teaching*. Edinburgh: Edinburgh University Press.

Petty, Geoff (2004). *Teaching Today*. Cheltenham: Nelson Thornes.

Pitt, Kathy (2005). *Debates in ESOL Teaching and Learning*. London: Routledge.

Portell, Sarah (2012). 'Teambuilding', in *English Teaching Professional*, Issue 80, pp. 9–10.

Prensky, M. (2001). *Digital Game-based Learning*. New York: McGraw-Hill.

Race, P. (1999). *2000 Tips for Lecturers*. London: Routledge.

Race, P. (2006). *The Lecturer's Toolkit: A Practical Guide to Assessment, Learning and Teaching*. Abingdon: Routledge.

Reinders, H. (2010). 'Towards a Classroom Pedagogy for Learner Autonomy: A Framework of Independent Language Learning Skills', *Australian Journal of Teacher Education*, 35(5): 40–55.

Reinders, Hayo and Lewis, Marilyn (2006). 'The Development of an Evaluative Checklist for Self-access Materials', *ELT Journal*, 60(2): 272–8.

Reinders, H. and Lewis, M. (2008). 'Materials Evaluation and Teacher Autonomy', in Lamb, T. and Reinders, H. (eds), *Learner and Teacher Autonomy: Realities and Responses*. Amsterdam: John Benjamins, pp. 205–16.

Reinders, H., Lewis, M. and Kirkness, A. (2010). *Good Teacher, Better Teacher. Strategies for the Multicultural Classroom*. Tokyo: Perceptia Press.

Reinders, H. and White, C. (2010). 'The Theory and Practice of Technology in Materials Development and Task Design', in Harwood, N. (ed.), *English Language Teaching Materials: Theory and Practice*. Cambridge: Cambridge University Press, pp. 58–80.

Richards, J. C. (2002). *Planning Aims and Objectives in Language Programs*, RELC Portfolio Series 5. Singapore: SEAMEO Regional Language Centre.

Richards, J. C. and Farrell, T. S. C. (2005). *Professional Development for Language Teachers*. Cambridge: Cambridge University Press.

Richards, Jack C. and Lockhart, Charles (1994). *Reflective Teaching in Second Language Classrooms*. Cambridge: Cambridge University Press.

Skibba, Karen (2013). 'Adult Learning Influence on Faculty Learning Cycle', in Keengwe, J. and Kyei-Blankson, L. (eds), *Virtual Mentoring for Teachers: Online Professional Development Practices*. Hershey, PA: Information Science Reference, pp. 263–91.

Slavin, R. E. (1990). *Collaborative Learning: Theory, Research and Practice*. Hillsdale, NJ: Prentice Hall.

Velez-Solic, Angela and Banas, Jennifer (2013). 'Professional Development for Online Educators', in Keengwe, J. and Kyei-Blankson, L. (eds), *Virtual Mentoring for Teachers: Online Professional Development Practices*. Hershey, PA: Information Science Reference, pp. 204–26.

Wigglesworth, Gillian (ed.) (2003). *The Kaleidoscope of Adult Second Language Learning: Learner, Teacher and Researcher Perspectives*. Sydney: Macquarie University.

Williams, M. and Burden, R. (1997). *Psychology for Language Teachers: A Social Constructivist Approach*. Cambridge: Cambridge University Press.

Index